Hollywood's Made to Order Punks

Part 2

A Pictorial History of:
The Dead End Kids
Little Tough Guys
East Side Kids
and
The Bowery Boys

by
Richard Roat

HOLLYWOOD'S MADE TO ORDER PUNKS / PART 2

By Richard Roat

Published in the USA by:
BearManor Media
P O Box 71426
Albany, Georgia 31708
www.bearmanormedia.com

ISBN: 978-1-59393-761-4
Printed in the United States of America
Book design by Robbie Adkins

CONTENTS

FOREWORD
by Mr. Eugene Francis, of the former East Side Kids

We usually arrived at the studios, on what was derisively called "Poverty Row," at seven a.m. They were ancient studios built in the heart of Hollywood. Actually, they were on Gower Street—often called "Gower Gulch" for the interiors of so many Low Budget Westerns were shot there.

Seven in the morning was painfully early for this Broadway Stage actor, but I was getting used to making my Hollywood film debut in a "quickie." This is what these "East Side Kid" films were called. Why "quickies?" Because the full length movie was to be shot in SIX days--sometimes on the SEVENTH if it had to go into overtime. Most films had a minimum four weeks shooting schedule and some features several months.

Our quickie was to be released by Monogram Studios. And the word in Movieland was if you worked for Monogram, you were either "on your way up or on your way down."

I replaced another actor who begged out when he got a job in a non-quickie. That was why I was cast in the first four films of the East Side Kids. There were only three actors from the original *Dead End* by Sidney Kingsley: the two Gorceys and Bobby Jordan. They not only appeared in the original Broadway play, but in the Warner Bros. prize-winning hit movie, which was certainly not a "quickie."

Sam Katzman, who was known as a producer who could make movies on the cheap, could have employed additional "*Dead End*" actors. Their contracts with Warner's had not been renewed and they all were available. He chose not to spend more money than was necessary.

I really learned my film craft from Bobby Jordan and Leo Gorcey, who had become quite adept in front of the camera, and above all Dave O'Brien, who aided me in learning the ropes.

In 1941 we knew nothing of television or residuals or DVDs, and if someone on Poverty Row had even hinted that 72-years later people would still be watching us, we would have said there must be a screw loose.

I had made only four of those quickies when the Army drafted me. I spent the next five years in uniform.

I may be the sole survivor of all of the original East Side Kids and, although I had worked for Monogram, I was actually on my way UP!

Eugene Francis
April 2013

FOREWORD
by Mr. Dick Chandlee, of the former East Side Kids

How could I ever have expected that working randomly in only one or two of the "Little Tough Guys" and "East Side Kids" movies decades ago would result in a recent invitation from Richard Roat to contribute a foreword to his latest publication of the lives and movie careers of a group of young movie tough guys who will always be known as the Dead End Kids. As you will see and read, Richard is their most dedicated fan and their most thorough, all-encompassing historian. He listens and looks everywhere for even the slightest connection to Dead End Kids' lives and movies and found even me.

The name, Dead End Kids, comes from their very successful central part in playwright Sidney Kingsley's 1935 hit Broadway play *Dead End*, about the interplay of a New York hoodlum kid street gang and local grown-ups living in a tenement neighborhood during the 1930s depression. In 1936, Sam Goldwyn, one of Hollywood's best known independent producers, saw the play, bought the film rights and produced the equally successful 1937 hit film *Dead End,* starring Humphrey Bogart, the ever-attractive Sylvia Sidney, Joel McCrea and Clare Trevor.

Because they sometimes could give an audience the impression they were real hoodlums collected off the street, the six original kids—Billy Halop (the gang leader), Leo Gorcey, Huntz Hall, Bobby Jordan, Gabriel Dell and Bernard Punsly—were given contracts and brought to Hollywood for the movie. During production of the film, the unique popularity of the Dead End Kid characters prompted Goldwyn to start looking for more street gang story ideas, but he abruptly gave it up when the Kids' off-screen, genuine "street-gang" behavior began extending the production schedule and budget. Their refusal to take making a movie seriously was too much for Goldwyn. When the film quickly showed success at the box office, Warner Bros., makers of some of the 1930s best crime and gangster films, made Goldwyn an offer to buy the Kids' contracts, which Goldwyn quickly accepted.

During 1938 and 1939, Warner Bros. made six films featuring the name "The Dead End Kids" at the top of the credits with Warner Bros.' stars. The first film, *Crime School* (1938), was to be the first of a Warner Bros. series, featuring "The Crime School Kids," but the name change proved disappointing to the public, who already wanted to see more of the original "Dead End Kids," and the idea was dropped. The most acclaimed of the six productions was *Angels with Dirty Faces* (1938), starring Humphrey Bogart and James Cagney as gangsters. Movie reviews praised the Kids as having attained star quality.

Also in 1938, Universal Pictures was preparing to produce their version of tough street kid stories. Universal was having financial difficulties at this time and kept only a limited number of stars under contract. They approached Warner's and worked out a deal to "borrow" the Kids for at least one street-gang story. The first of these films, *Little Tough Guy,* used only four of the Kids: Billy Halop, Huntz Hall, Gabriel Dell and Bernard Punsly. Leo Gorcey and Bobby Jordan were being withheld by Warner's for separate work in other Warner films and were also getting outside film work. Universal replaced them with two capable tough-guy substitutes: Halley Chester and David Gorcey, Leo's younger brother. This was the first working breakup of the original six Kids, which turned out to happen frequently from then on.

The publicity and screen credits for the medium-budget *Little Tough Guy* movie made no mention of "Dead End Kids" in the cast. They were publicized and presented only as Universal's *Little Tough Guy* gang. The 1938 film received good reviews and did well enough at the box office for Universal to go ahead with a film series featuring their "Little Tough

Guys". The next three films were cast without any Dead End Kids, only with the newly assembled "Little Tough Guys" gang: Harris Berger, Halley Chester, Charles Duncan, Billy Benedict and David Gorcey. But disappointing box office results for all three movies prompted Universal to remake the deal with Warner's and adjust the film schedule to make sure there were Dead End Kids in each of the following films. Members of the two gangs were merged and the featured name of the series was changed to read in big type: "THE DEAD END KIDS and Little Tough Guys".

During 1939, Universal got a break when Warner's finished *On Dress Parade,* the sixth production starring The Dead End Kids, decided not to make any more and dropped the Kids' contracts. Universal was now able to sign Halop, Hall, Dell, Punsly and later on, Bobby Jordan, to continue with their Dead-End-Tough-Guy series. All together, between 1938 and 1943, Universal made twelve features and three Saturday-afternoon serials with production interlaced, at first, with Warner Bros.' six-movie production schedule and with a merging of Dead End Kids and Little Tough Guys gang members. The series came to an end in 1943 when Billy Halop, who had the leading role of gang leader, was drafted into the Army and replaced by Bobby Jordan in the final film, *Keep 'Em Slugging.* Thus, the Kids, with their Dead-End gang celebrity, had achieved a remarkable level of movie success: being featured in two film series simultaneously at two different studios.

In late 1939, Sam Katzman, a veteran low-budget film producer, contacted Monogram Pictures, a small, low-budget film studio on the east side of Hollywood, and sold the studio on a street gang film series designed to take advantage of the current box office popularity of the Dead End Kids and Little Tough Guys. The films would be typically low budget with a shooting schedule of seven days maximum and total production costs of around $35,000 (in 1939 dollars)—about half of what a major studio would spend on a usual outdoor cowboy movie. Katzman made an effort to get at least one or two of the Dead End Kids for lead roles but, at that time, none were interested in the low-budget offer or were tied to other commitments. In lieu of Dead End Kids, Katzman hired Little Tough Guys' Halley Chester and Harris Berger, along with five other new, young, tough-guy actors to form a new gang. The first film, entitled *East Side Kids,* was released on February 10, 1940, but did only so-so at the box office without the name, *Dead End Kids,* on the marquee.

There were five months between *East Side Kids* and the second film, *Boys of the City,* and good things happened. Bobby Jordan became available, followed shortly afterward by pugnacious Leo Gorcey, who was given the central part of pugnacious Ethelbert "Muggs" McGinnis, the gang's leader. Jordan was given the role of Muggs's close sidekick, young Danny Nolan. Katzman hired African-American Ernest "Sunshine Sammy" Morrison to play the running part of Scruno. Morrison's acting career began when he was still a babe-in-arms, and blossomed in 1922 when comedy producer Hal Roach selected him as one of the original members of the first *Our Gang* comedy shorts. Back-up members of the *East Side Kids* gang changed from film to film and consisted mostly of Little Tough Guy gang members. In 1941, Huntz Hall rejoined the gang as "Glimpy," a minor character to begin with, but whose talent for comedy and interplay with Gorcey's "Muggs" began shifting the series away from serious street dramas toward lighter comedy themes.

A total of 21 *East Side Kids* films were made and released between 1940 and 1945. The end came when Leo Gorcey, whose "Muggs" character was essentially the star of the series, told producer Sam Katzman he wanted his contract salary doubled. Katzman refused. Gorcey quit the series on the spot and Katzman ended the series on the spot. When the shock settled, Bobby Jordan, Huntz Hall and Leo Gorcey met with Gorcey's agent, Jan Grippo, who recommended they form their own production company, based on a reworked version of *The East Side Kids* with an emphasis on comedy. The name of the series would be *The Bowery Boys.* Gorcey's "Muggs" character was now Aloysius "Slip" Mahoney and Huntz Hall's "Glimpy" became Horace Debussy "Sach" Jones. Bobby Jordan's character remained straight "Bobby." The new company was named Jan Grippo Productions, with Gorcey having a forty percent interest. With positive approval from Monogram Pictures, *Live Wires,* the first of 48 Bowery Boys films, was completed and released in January 1946. The final film, *In the Money,* was released by Monogram in February 1958.

In the 1960s and 1970s, the *East Side Kids* and *Bowery Boys* series collected a new generation of fans when they were syndicated for television. DVDs are also available, so keep looking.

Dick "Stash" Chandlee
August 26, 2013

FOREWORD
by Mr. David Gorcey, III (grandson of David Gorcey)

The memories I have of my grandfather are as a kind, endearing person with what I now realize is a bit of New York snark, toning it way back to just be a happy grandfather when I was around him. I enjoyed his visits as a child and truly wish there could have been more. If he were alive today, he'd probably be a lot of fun to spend a night on the town with and he'd probably still find a way to capture the attention of the prettiest women in the room.

From a higher level, his life was a bit more complicated. Hollywood was different in his days, just like everything else was. Establishing a career in entertainment was harder—there were fewer movies being made, TV was still relatively new, and the phrase "viral sensation" back then had an entirely different meaning. I think it's unfortunate that we never really got to see what my grandfather was fully capable of as an entertainer. His roles in the Bowery Boys/Dead End Kids/Little Tough Guys movies didn't see him with many lines and his career was mostly dependent on, and intertwined with, that of his brother Leo's. This seems to have ultimately complicated his quest to find his own way in the business following the series of movies he's best known for, though it didn't prevent him from getting parts here and there with guys like Abbott & Costello.

In the end, he seems to have had the desire to be a positive force in the world by helping people with substance abuse problems, and playing a part in his son's family, however late to the game he may have been on that. He loved to tell a good story but when it mattered, he always called them like he saw them, and would want for you to do the same about him. So in keeping true to that, David Gorcey, my grandfather, was fortunate enough to have a movie career in a time where that really meant something in Hollywood, and there's not too many people who can say that. It's too bad we didn't get to see him do more with his talents, and it's too bad that his life had some of the distractions that it did. But we'll always have his movies, and I'll always have a name that occasionally causes someone to ask if I'm related to the Bowery Boys guys, although, let's be honest, they're usually asking about Leo. Either way, I think it's pretty cool. Thanks, grandpa!

Cheers,
David

DEDICATION

Dedicated to the memories of the actors who were the Dead End Kids/Little Tough Guys/East Side Kids and the Bowery Boys, also to Buddy Gorman (September 2nd, 1921-April 1st, 2010), Mendie Koenig (May 24th, 1918,-January, 4th, 2013).

Also, to my dear wife Mary, daughter Jenny, and in loving memory of my mom and dad. And special thanks to my nephew Phil Howell for his work with the pictures in this book.

NOTE:

All pictures in this book are from author's personal collection.

INTRODUCTION

A little background on the Dead End Kids, Little Tough Guys, East Side Kids and the Bowery Boys, before, as Slip would say, you peruse the pages in this book.

In 1935 there were a number of Broadway plays that opened and closed after only a few performances. One such play was *Waiting for Lefty* (starring Luther Adler and Elia Kazan), which closed after only 24 performances.

On the other hand, *Three Men on a Horse*, which opened on Broadway at the Playhouse Theatre on January 30, ran for over 800 performances. Another play that opened on Broadway at the Belasco Theatre in 1935 was called *Dead End* (written by Sidney Kingsley), which had a run of 687 performances, opening on October 28 and closing two years later on June 12, 1937.

"What made the play *Dead End* different than any other play on Broadway?

For one thing, the dialog that the six Dead End Kids spoke was rough (gezz the nuts, dess n dem) and the setting of the play was not what theater audience were used to. The backdrop of the play told the story of poverty and the ruthless life of the streets.

When *Dead End* premiered on October 28, 1935, audiences were taken aback with the language that spewed from the six young actors' mouths— they were "The Dead End Kids," and forever they would remain the Dead End Kids. Some 78 years later, they are just as popular as they were in 1935.

Bernard Punsly (Milty), Gabriel Dell (T.B.), Huntz Hall (Dippy), Bobby Jordan (Angel) Leo Gorcey (Spit) and Billy Halop (Tommy) took Broadway by storm.

Fast forward to 2013, seventy eight years later. There have been four books written on the kids: *The Films of the Bowery Boys*, by Walker Hayes; *From Broadway to the Bowery*, by Len Getz; *Hollywood's Made to Order Punks*, by Richard Roat; and the last one being *Beyond Dead End*, by Joseph Fusco.

Besides the books that have been written about the kids and their lives on and off the screen, there have been three revivals of the play *Dead End*, the last one being at the Griffith Theater in Chicago (2006).

There are a number of websites and Facebook pages solely devoted to the Kids.

Each new year brings new fans.

This is their story in picture form, from the play *Dead End* to their last film, *In the Money*, done in 1958. I hope you enjoy your journey while you thumb through the pictures of their lives.

CHAPTER 1
The play *Dead End*
Where it all began

Opening Night
October 28, 1935

Cast: Babyface Martin (Joseph Dowing), Mrs. Martin (Marjorie Main), Hunk (Martin Gabel, Kay (Margaret Mullen), Gimpy (Ted Newton), TB (Gabriel Dell), Spit (Charles R. Duncan), Angel (Bobby Jordan), Dippy (Huntz Hall), Tommy (Billy Halop), Milty (Bernard Punsly), Francey (Sheila Trent), 2nd Ave. Boys (David and Leo Gorcey)

Author's Notes: The play *Dead End* was the longest running play at the Belasco Theatre, a record that still stands today.

Once Samuel Goldwyn purchased the film rights to the play *Dead End.* the six Dead End Kids were off to Hollywood to reprise their stage roles.

Charles Duncan by rights should have been a star, but it was his misfortune that he only become a footnote.

The role of Spit in the play Dead End was his, he had the looks—a sneer with a venomous look—but it wasn't to be.

Duncan was born in Kentucky on March 12, 1920. He acted in a few plays in high school. After graduating, he set his sights on the New York stage—Broadway. After knocking around New York for about two months and getting nowhere fast, he answered a casting call for young actors between the ages of eleven and twenty. With a group of about thirty kids, including Eugene Francis (who later went on to become an East Side Kid), he was told he wasn't what they were looking for. Being somewhat discouraged but knowing he was a good actor, he tried again, and this time he was cast in the play *Dead End*, in one of the title roles of the play as Spit. After only playing the much sought after role of Spit for three months, and being signaled out by critics for his lasting portrayal of a hood in the making, he contracted pneumonia, which, in 1935, was the kiss of death. His contract was bought out with three months of salary given. In walks Leo B. Gorcey as Duncan's understudy. Gorcey was originally cast along with younger brother David as a 2nd Ave. Boy. Once well again, Duncan was cast in the play *Bright Honor*. Sadly, it closed after seventeen performances.

Knocking on doors and getting no parts, Duncan headed off to California in 1937, found an agent and was cast in the Universal series the *Little Tough Guys*, becoming a Little Tough Guy in three films. At the outset of World War II (1940), Duncan enlisted in the U.S. Air Force. He was killed in action as an air gunner in 1942.

Dead End Manuscript

Original Cover of the playbill for the play Dead End used until 12-35

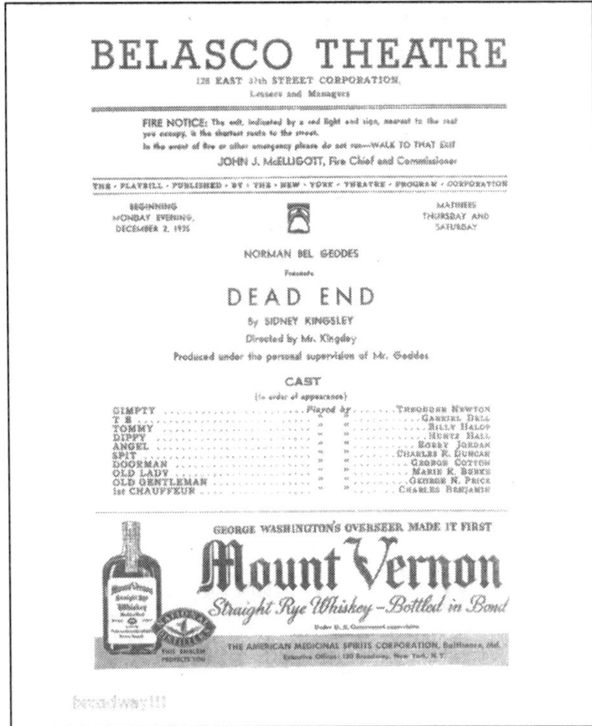

BELASCO THEATRE

128 EAST 37th STREET CORPORATION,
Lessees and Managers

FIRE NOTICE: The exit, indicated by a red light and sign, nearest to the seat you occupy, is the shortest route to the street.
In the event of fire or other emergency please do not run—WALK TO THAT EXIT
JOHN J. McELLIGOTT, Fire Chief and Commissioner

THE · PLAYBILL · PUBLISHED · BY · THE · NEW · YORK · THEATRE · PROGRAM · CORPORATION

BEGINNING MONDAY EVENING, DECEMBER 2, 1935

MATINEES THURSDAY AND SATURDAY

NORMAN BEL GEDDES

Presents

DEAD END

By SIDNEY KINGSLEY

Directed by Mr. Kingsley

Produced under the personal supervision of Mr. Geddes

CAST

(In order of appearance)

GIMPTY .... Played by .... Theodore Newton
T B .... " " .... Gabriel Dell
TOMMY .... " " .... Billy Halop
DIPPY .... " " .... Huntz Hall
ANGEL .... " " .... Bobby Jordan
SPIT .... " " .... Charles R. Duncan
DOORMAN .... " " .... George Cotton
OLD LADY .... " " .... Marie R. Burke
OLD GENTLEMAN .... " " .... George N. Price
1st CHAUFFEUR .... " " .... Charles Benjamin

Playbill of the play Dead End,listing Charles Duncan in the credits

Interior shot of the play Dead End

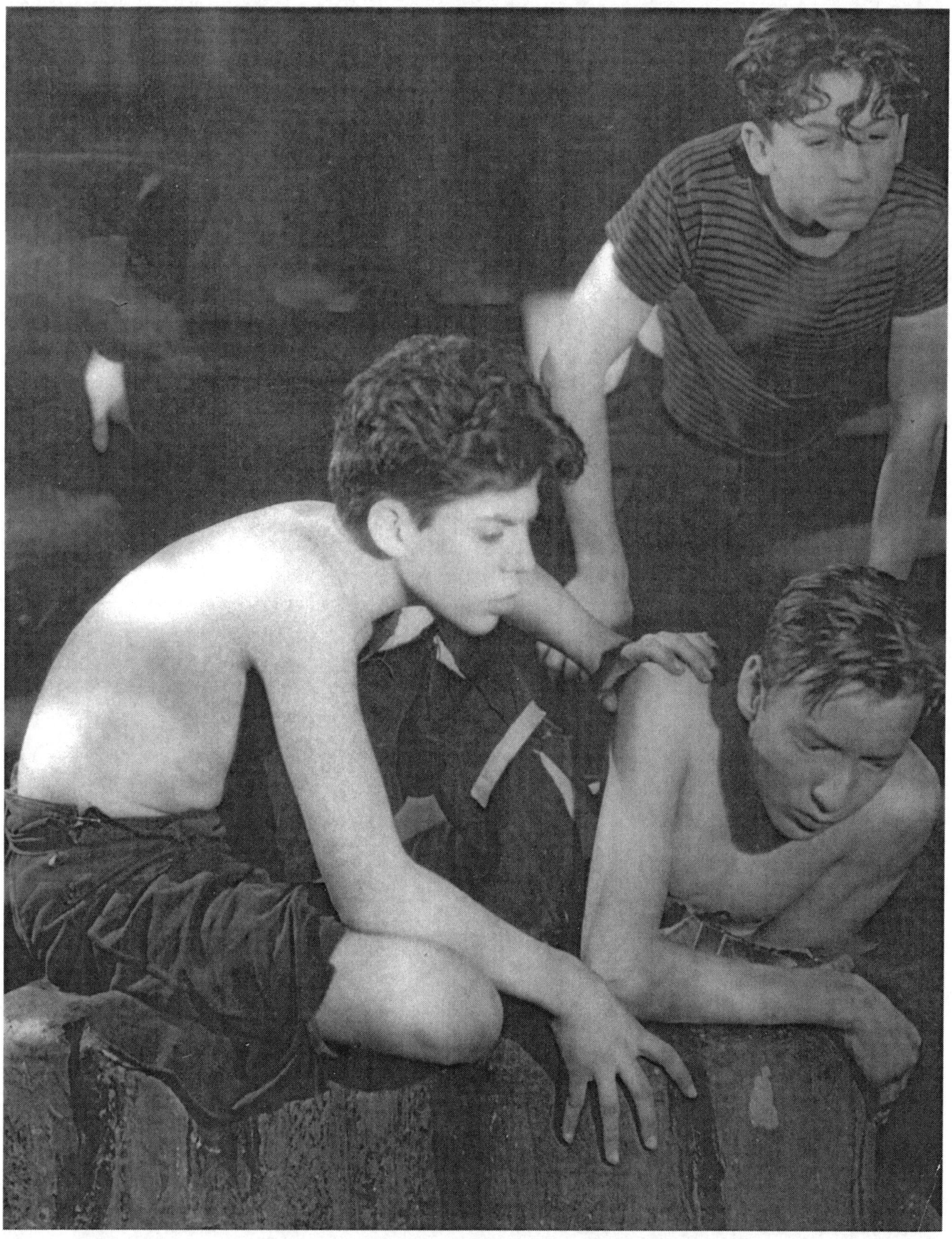

Publicity still of Billy Halop, Gabe Dell and Huntz Hall

Scene from the play Dead End,Billy Halop has Charles Duncan in his grasp

Scene shot of the play Dead End

The Dead End Kids have a Christmas Party back stage,on the set of the play Dead End

CHAPTER 2
The films of the Dead End Kids—1937-1939 with the original Dead End Kids

Dead End

Samuel Goldwyn: Released, August 27, 1937

Cast: Humphrey Bogart, Sylvia Sidney, Joel McCrea, Marjorie Main, Claire Trevor, Wendy Barrie and the Dead End Kids (Bernard Punsly, Gabriel Dell, Bobby Jordan, Leo Gorcey, Billy Halop, Huntz Hall)

Autographed photo from Dead End by Sylvia Sidney and Joel McCrea

The mark of the squealer

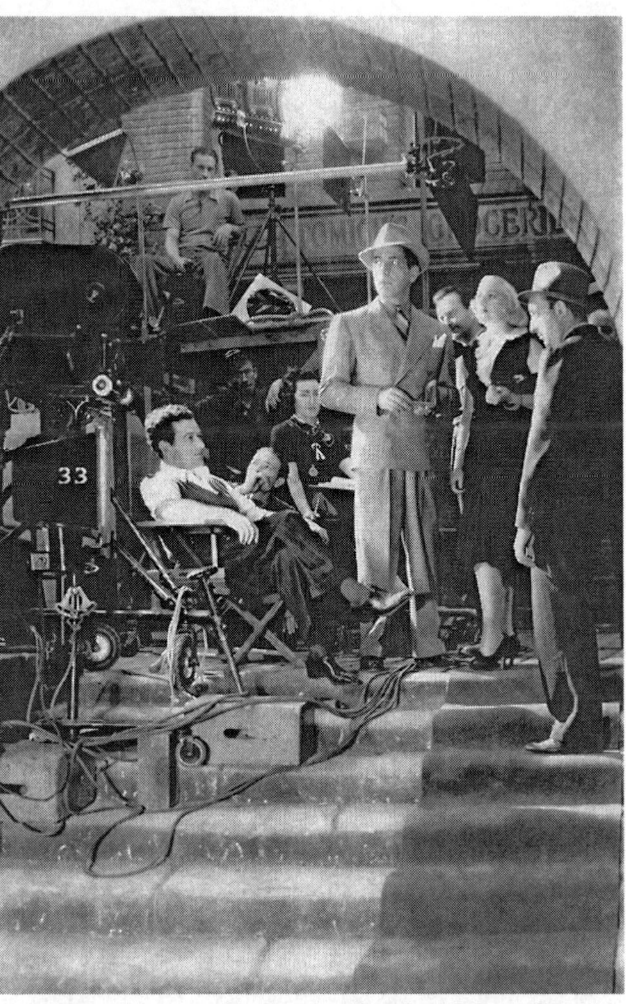

Bogart waiting to film a scene for the film Dead End

Scene from Dead End

Cap-Charles Peck tells it like it is

Cap-Joel McCrae in Dead Endand Joel McCrea

Portrait of
Sylvia Sidney

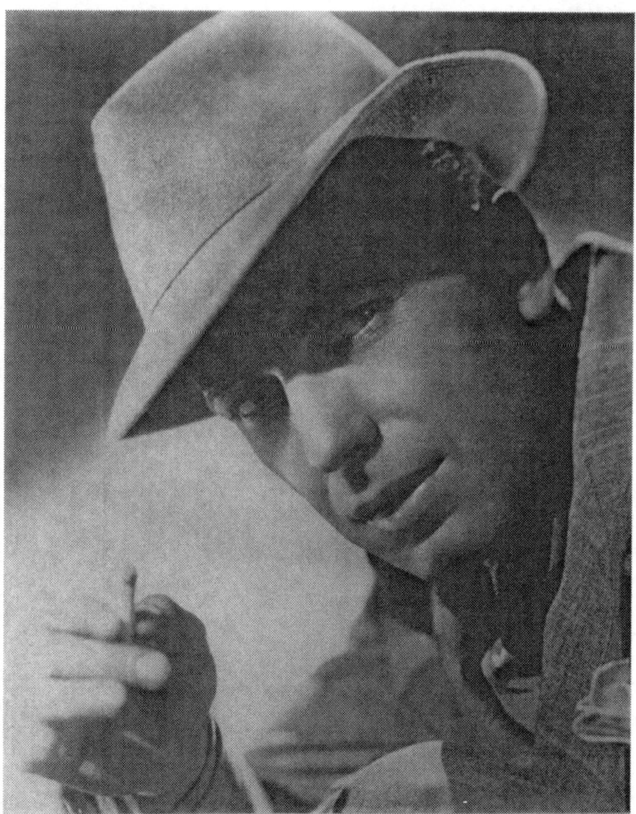

Portrait still-Bogart in Dead End

Sylvia and Joel McCrea as they appeared in Dead End

Crime School

Warner Bros.: Released, May 28, 1938

Cast: Humphrey Bogart, Gale Page, Cy Kendall, Weldon Heyburn, George Offerman Jr. and the Dead End Kids

I'm not goin

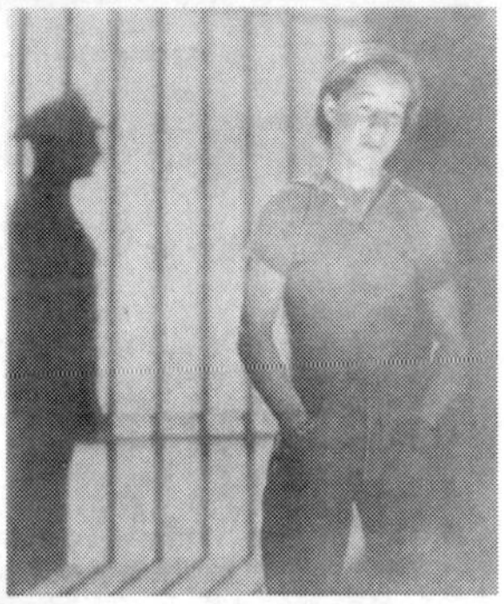

Portrait of Bobby Jordan

Lobby Card for Crime School

Cap-Gorcey and Halop-fighting

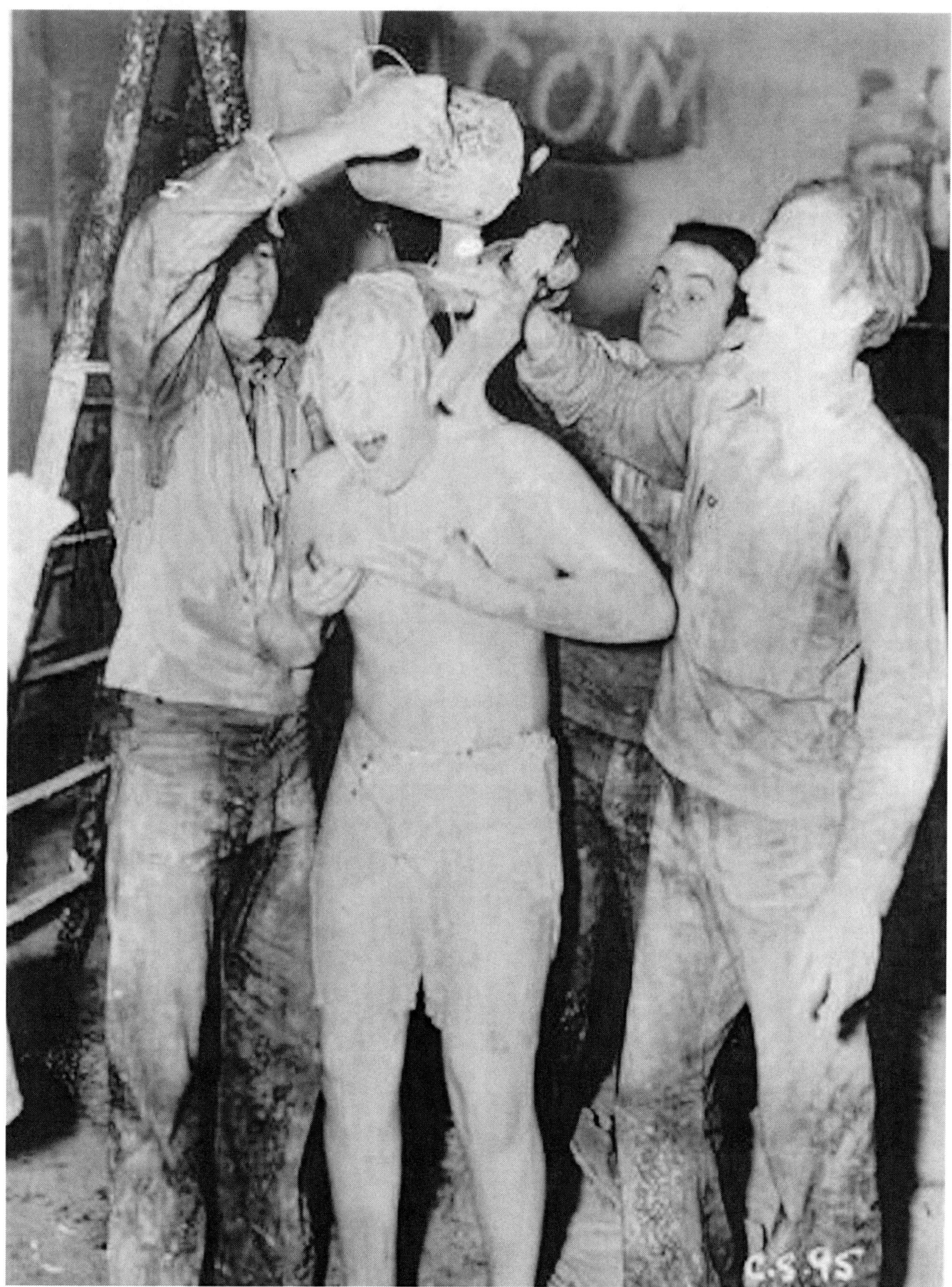

Crime School-punsly-white wash me

I think im gonna be sick

Lobby Card with Bogart and Leo Gorcey

Who's goin wit me

Put down that rock

Half Sheet poster

Publicity still of Gabe Dell, Huntz Hall and Humphrey Bogart

Insert for the film Crime School

Angels With Dirty Faces

Warner Bros.: Released November 24, 1938

Cast: James Cagney, Ann Sheridan, Pat O'Brien, Humphrey Bogart, George Bancroft, the Dead End Kids and Frankie Burke

Lobby Card for Angels With Dirty Faces

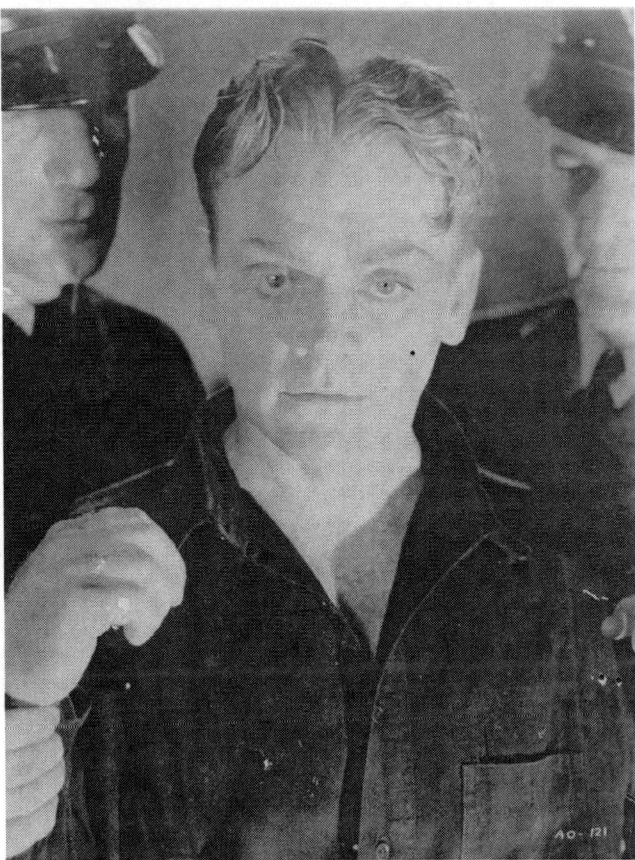

Original still of James Cagney in Angels With Dirty Faces,walks to the chair

Bogart in Angels With Dirty Faces

Pat O'Brian and Billy Halop in this publicity still

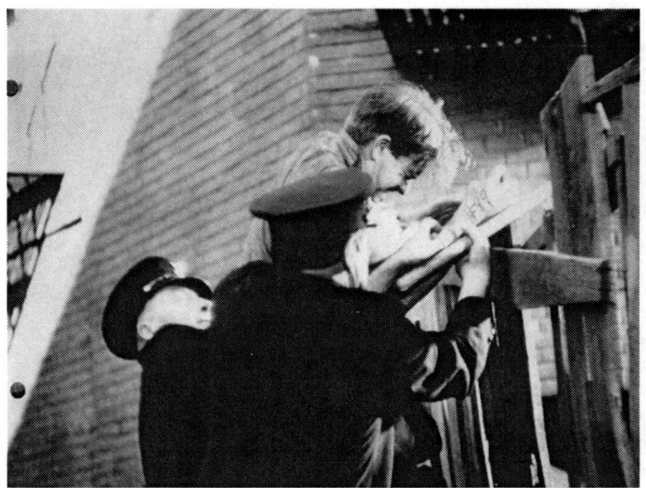

Frankie Burke-being caught by police in this scene from Angels With Dirty Faces

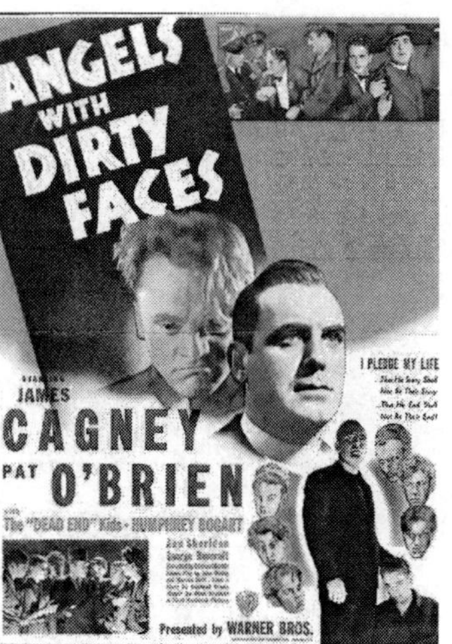

One Sheet Poster for Angels With Dirty Faces

Pat O'Brian portrait still

Laury an Rocky in this scene

Father Jerry and Rocky check out there old digs

Rocky receives last rites

The Kids with Cagney

William Tracy and Frankie Burke are ready to make a run for it

Rocky waiting to be called to take his last walk to the Electric Chair

Whata hear whata ya say

Leo Gorcey and James Cagney-I did'nt say a word

They Made Me a Criminal

Warner Bros.: Released January 28, 1939

Cast: John Garfield, Gloria Dickson, Ann Sheridan, Claude Rains, May Robson, the Dead End Kids and Ward Bond

Ann Sheridan and John Garfield in a posed shot from They Made Me a Criminal

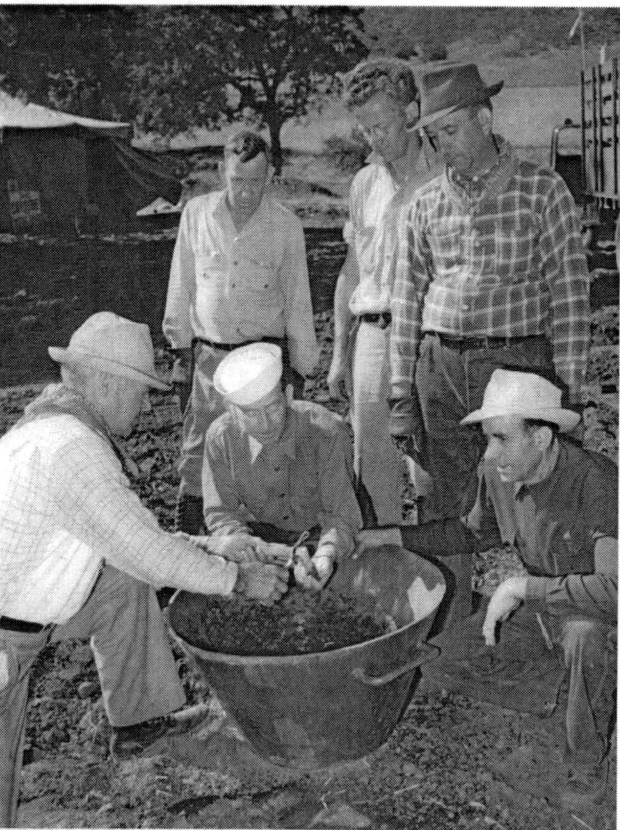

Crew workers prepare dinner on the set of They Made Me a Criminal

You Big Lummox

I told you no Pictures

Aw Peggy

Garfield, Halop

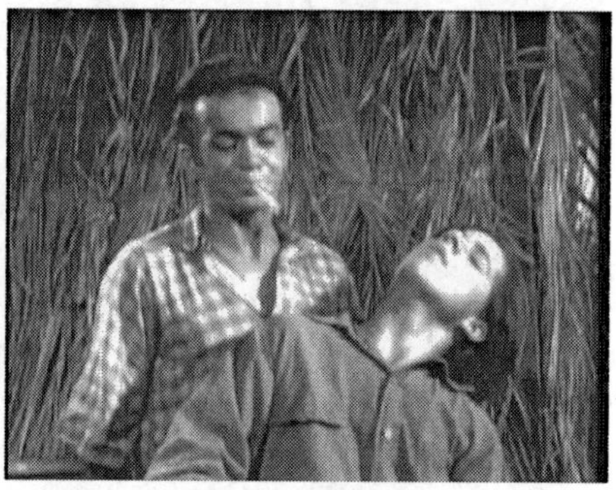

Spitting contest

The Dead End Kids and Gloria Dickson in a scene from They Made Me a Criminal

Portrait of John Garfield relaxing on the set of They Made Me a Criminal

Lobby Card for They Made Me a Criminal

Look what just blew in

Scene from They Made Me a Criminal

Hell's Kitchen

Warner Bros.: Released July 8, 1939

Cast: Ronald Reagan, Margaret Lindsey, Stanley Fields, Grant Mitchell and the Dead End Kids

Hell's Kitchen Poster

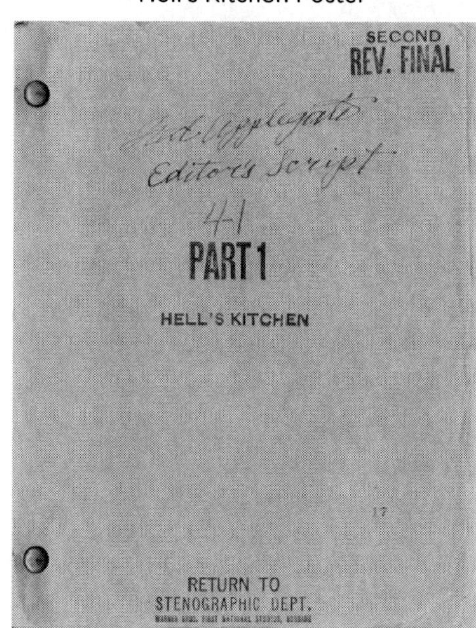

Editors script-Hell's Kitchen

Ronald Reagan, Margart Lindsey and Bobby Jordan

Billy Halop and Leo Gorcey

A very rare still

Bobby Jordan in a publicity still for Hell's Kitchen

The Angels Wash Their Faces

Warner Bros.: Released August 26, 1939

Working Title: Battle of City Hall

Cast: Ann Sheridan, Ronald Reagan, Eduardo Ciannelli, Henry O'Neill, Berton Churchill, Grady Sutton, Frankie Thomas, Frankie Burke, Frankie Coghlan and the Dead End Kids.

Ann Sherdian Billy Halop and Ronald Reagan in this scene from Angels Wash Their Faces

Scene for Angels Wash Their Faces

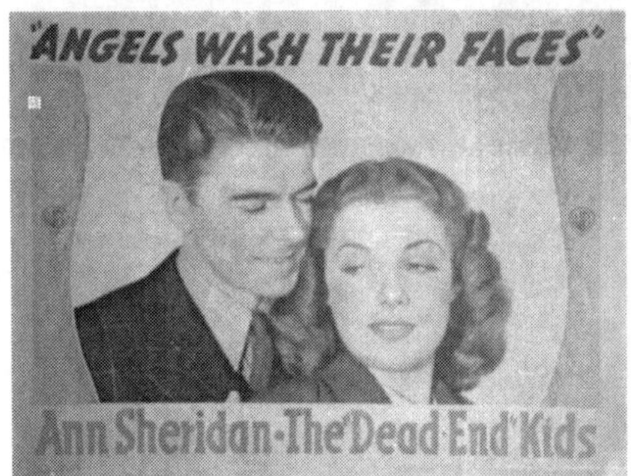

"ANGELS WASH THEIR FACES"
Ann Sheridan-The Dead End Kids

Lobby Card for Angels Wash Their Faces

Angels Wash Their faces-still

Bonita Granville and Majorie Main in a scene from Angels Wash Thier Faces

One sheet poster for Angels Wash Their Faces

ANN SHERIDAN
and THE DEAD END KIDS
in
"ANGELS WASH THEIR FACES"
RONALD REAGAN
GRANVILLE THOMAS O'NEILL CIANNELLI
DIRECTED by RAY ENRIGHT
Presented by WARNER BROS.

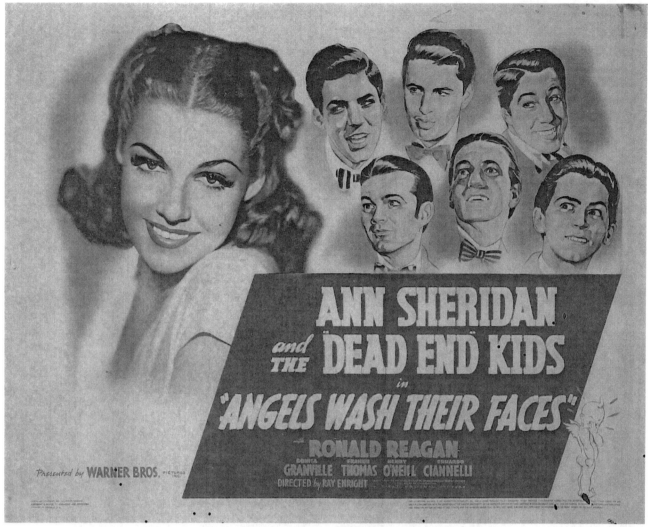

Angels Wash Their Faces lobby card

Scene for Angels Wash Their Faces

Scene for Angels Wash Their Faces

On Dress Parade

Warner Bros.: Released November 18, 1939

Cast: John Litel, Frankie Thomas and the Dead End Kids

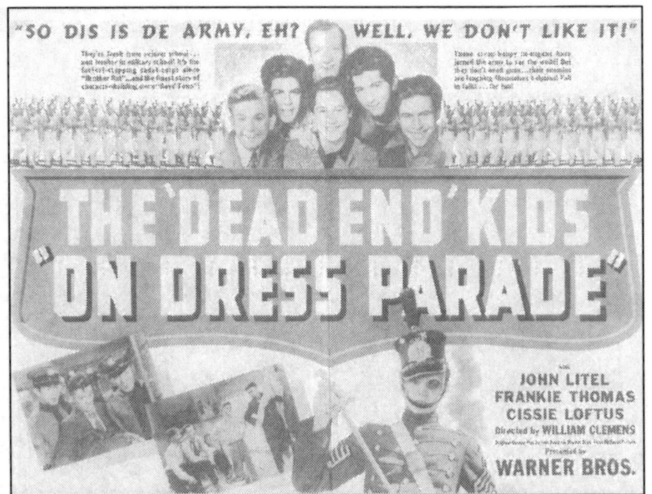

Lobby card from On Dress Parade

Billy Halop in a scene from On Dress Parade

Glass slide for On Dress Parade

Lobby Card from the film On Dress Parade

On Dress Parade one sheet poster

Scene still from On Dress Parade

Scene from On Dress Parade

On Dress Parade lobby card

CHAPTER 3
The Universal years 1938-1943
The Dead End Kids and Little Tough Guy years

Little Tough Guy

Universal Studios: Released July 22, 1938

<u>Cast</u>: Robert Wilcox, Marjorie Main, Ed Pawley, Charles Trowbridge, Helen Parrish, Peggy Stewart, Jackie Searl, as the Dead End Kids, Billy Halop, Huntz Hall, Gabriel Dell, Bernard Punsly, and as Little Tough Guys, David Gorcey and Hally Chester.

Press photo of the Little Tough Guys

Huntz Hall, Hally Chester and Gabe Dell in this publicty still for Little Tough Guy

All 8 lobby cards for Little Tough Guy

Lobby card for Little Tough Guy

Publicity still for the film Little Tough Guy

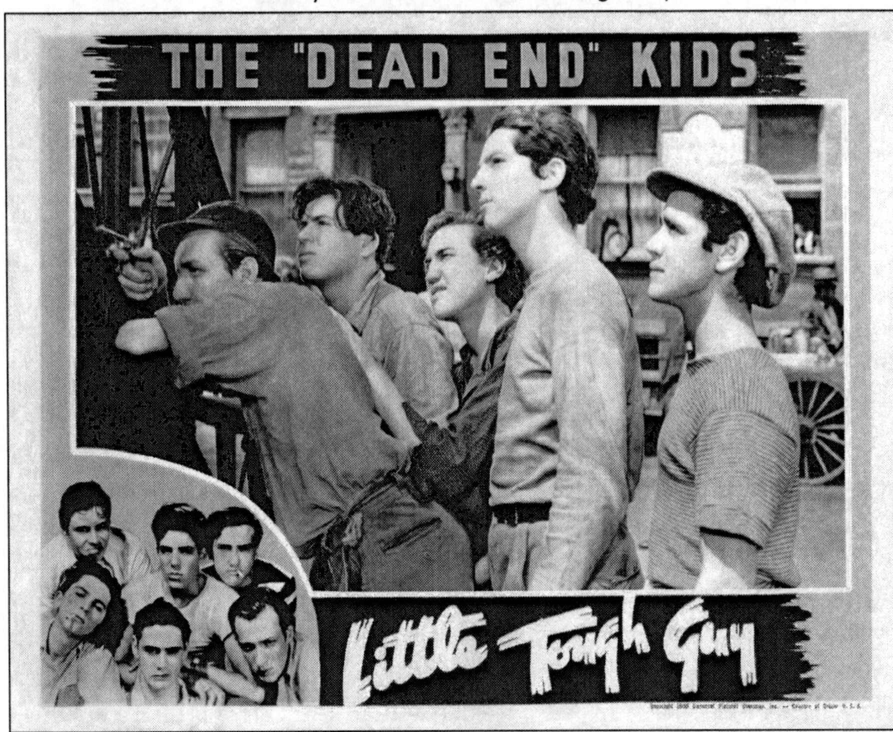

David Gorcey far right in -Little Tough Guy

Hally Chester and Bernard Punsly in this shot from Little Tough Guy

Jackie Searl,David Gorcey and Hunz Hall

Publicity still of the Dead End Kids for the film Little Tough Guy

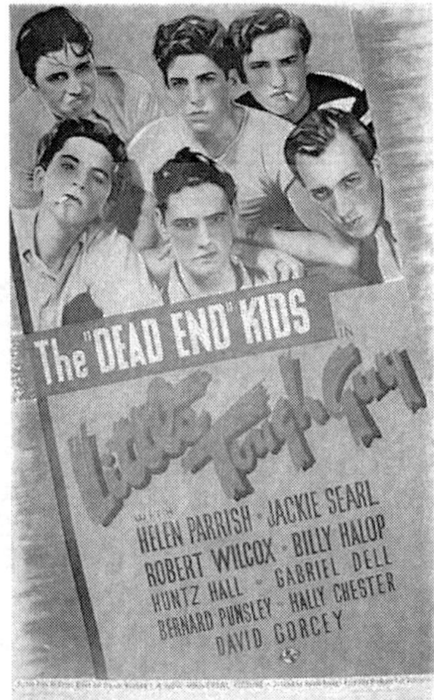

Little Tough Guy one sheet poster

Call a Messenger:

Universal Studios: Released November 3, 1939

Cast: Larry "Buster" Crabbe, Robert Armstrong, Victor Jory, Mary Carlisle, Anne Nagel, Jimmy Butler, El Brendel, as the Dead End Kids, Billy Halop and Huntz Hall, and as the Little Tough Guys, Billy Benedict, David Gorcey, Hally Chester and Harris Berger.

El Brendel and Billy Halop in a scene from Call a Messenger

Billy Halop and Victor Jory in a scene from Call a Messenger

Call a Messenger scene still

Scene from Call a Messenger

Call a Messenger still

Billy Halop,Mary Carlisle and Buster Crabbe in this publicity still

Call a Messenger insert

Lobby Card from Call a Messenger

Poster for Call a Messenger

You're Not So Tough

Universal Studios: Released July 26, 1940

<u>Cast</u>: Nan Grey, Rosina Galli, Henry Armetta, as the Dead End Kids, Billy Halop, Bobby Jordan, Huntz Hall, Bernard Punsly and Gabe Dell. Playing the Little Tough Guys were David Gorcey, Harris Berger and Hally Chester.

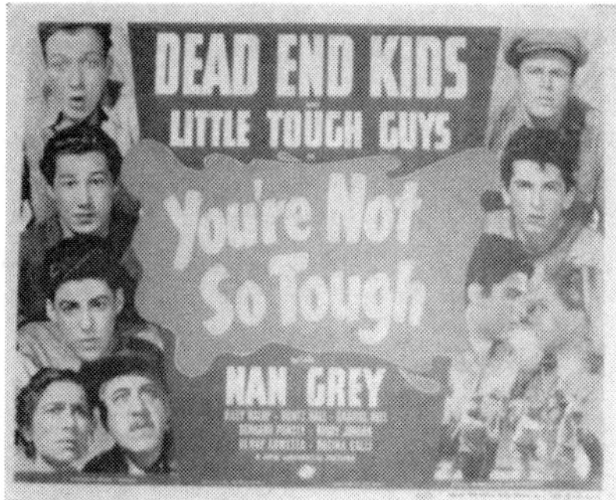

Title lobby card for You're not So Tough

Billy Halop and Nan Grey

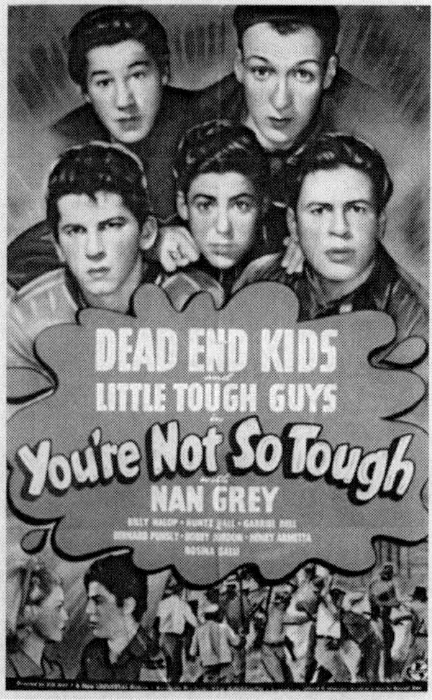

Poster for You're Not So Tough

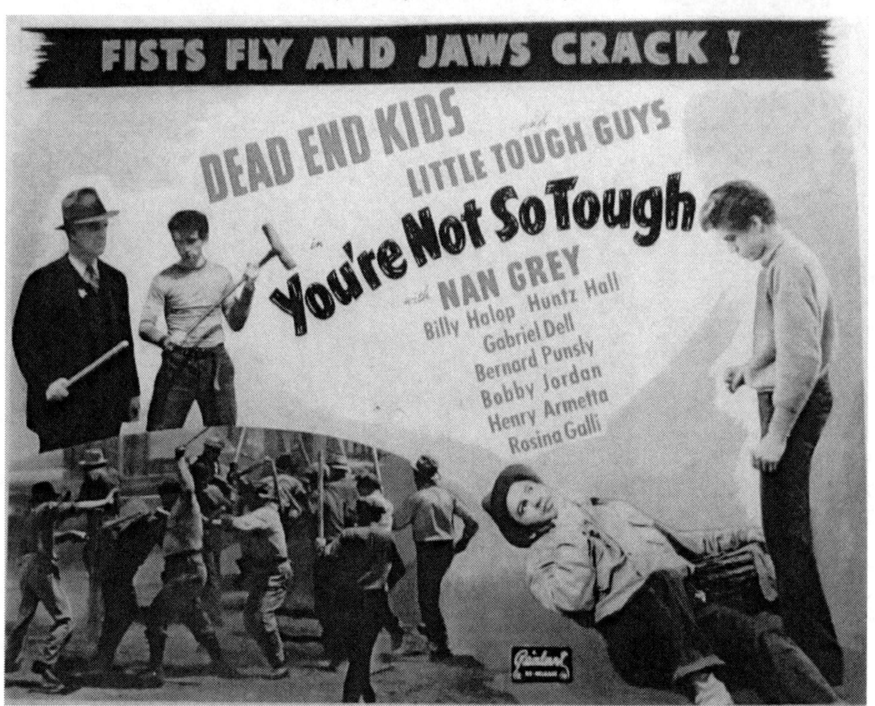

Lobby Card for You're Not So Tough

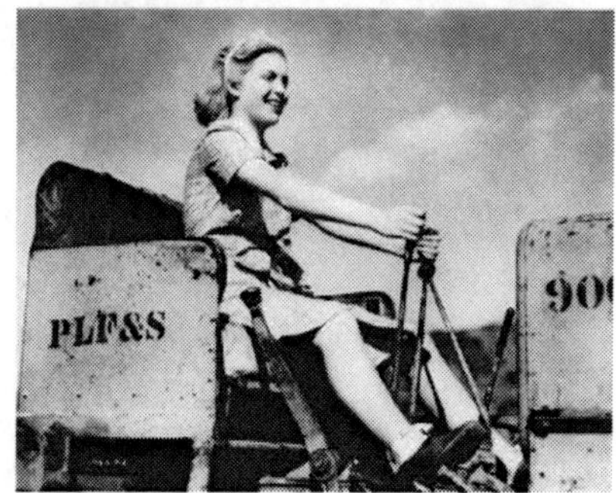

Nan Grey i this publicity still for the film You're Not So Tough

Junior G-Men (a twelve-chapter serial)

Universal Studios: Released August 1940
Chapter 1 "Enemies Within"
Chapter 2 "The Blast of Doom"
Chapter 3 "Human Dynamite"
Chapter 4 "Blazing Danger"
Chapter 5 "Trapped by Traitors"
Chapter 6 "Traitor's Treachery"
Chapter 7 "Flaming Death"
Chapter 8 "Hurled Through Space"
Chapter 9 "The Plunge of Peril"
Chapter 10 "The Toll of Treason"
Chapter 11 "Descending Doom"
Chapter 12 "The Power of Patriotism"

Cast: Phillip Terry, Cy Kendall, as the Dead End Kids, Billy Halop, Gabe Dell, Huntz Hall, Bernard Punsly, and as the Little Tough Guys, Hally Chester, Harris Berger.

Billy Halop and Huntz Hall in Jr. G-Men

Chapter
7
"FLAMING DEATH"
DEAD END KIDS
LITTLE TOUGH GUYS
JUNIOR
G-MEN

Chapter 7 Jr. G-Men Lobby Card

Jr.G-Men lobby card

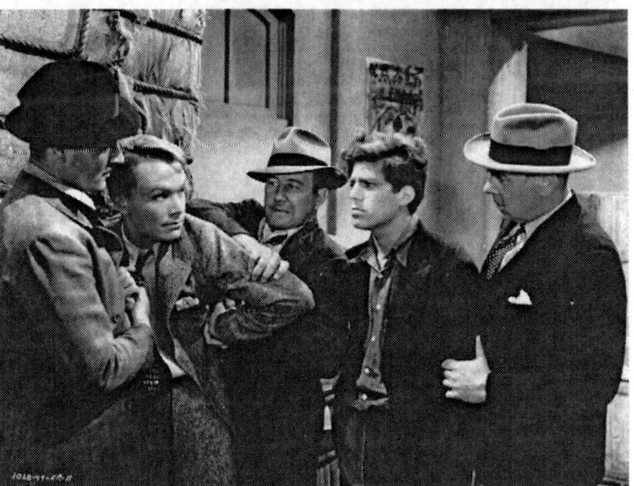

Scene still from Jr. G-Men

Scene for the 12 chapter Serial Jr. G-Men

One sheet poster

Give Us Wings

Universal Studios: Released December 20, 1940

Cast: Wallace Ford, Anne Gwynne, Milburn Stone, Shemp Howard, the Dead End Kids, and as the Little Tough Guys, Billy Benedict and Harris Berger.

Publicity Still from Give Us Wings

Ann Gwynne portrait for the film Give Us Wings

Billy Halop and Anne Gwynne in this publicity still

Press book for the film Give Us Wings

Bobby Jordan in the film Give Us Wings

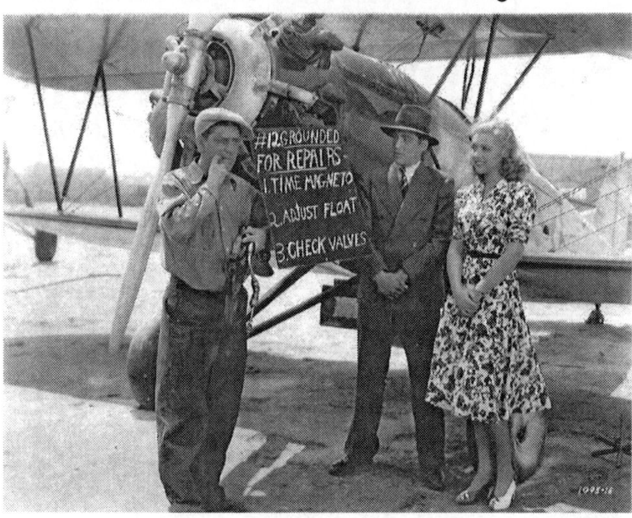

Shemp Howard, Billy Halop and Anne Gwynne in a scene from Give Us Wings

Publicity still for Give Us Wings-with Billy Halop, Anne Gwynne and Wallace Ford

Give Us Wings lobby card

One sheet poster for Give Us Wings

Hit the Road

Universal Studios: Released June 27, 1941

Cast: Gladys George, Barton MacLane, Evelyn Ankers, Shemp Howard, Bobs Watson, Hally Chester and the Dead End Kids.

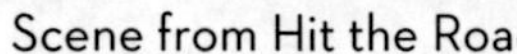

Scene from Hit the Road

Lobby card for Hit the Road

Scene from Hit the Road autographed by Bobs Watson

Scene from Hit the Road

Scene from Hit the Road

Hit the Road one sheet poster

Sea Raiders (a twelve-chapter serial)

Universal Studios: Released August 1941

Chapter 1 "The Raider Strikes"
Chapter 2 "Flaming Torture"
Chapter 3 "The Tragic Crash"
Chapter 4 "The Raider Strikes Again"
Chapter 5 "Flames of Fury"
Chapter 6 "Blasted from the Air"
Chapter 7 "Victims of the Storm"
Chapter 8 "Dragged to Their Doom"
Chapter 9 "Battling the Beast"
Chapter 10 "Periled by a Panther"
Chapter 11 "Entombed in a Tunnel"
Chapter 12 "Paying the Penalty"

Cast: John McGuire, Mary Field, Reed Hadley, Hally Chester and the Dead End Kids.

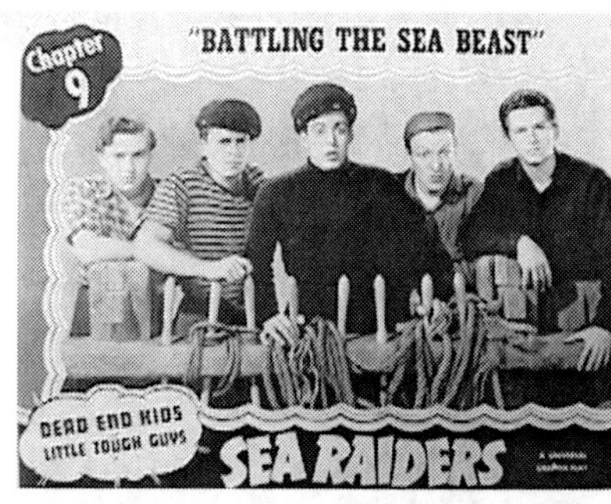

Sea Raiders-chapter 9 lobby card

One sheet poster from chapter 11

Billy Halop in scene from Sea Raiders

Poster for Chapter 3

Scene from Sea Raiders

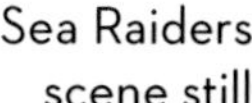

Sea Raiders scene still

4 scenes from Sea Raiders

Mob Town

Universal Studios: Released October 3, 1941

Cast: Dick Foran, Anne Gwynne, Darryl Hickman, the Dead End Kids and Hally Chester

Title lobby card for the film Mob Town

Scene from the film Mob Town

Mob Town insert

Mob Town one sheet poster

Junior G-Men of the Air (a twelve-chapter serial)

Universal Studios: Released June 1942

Chapter 1 "Wings Aflame"

Chapter 2 "The Plunge of Peril"

Chapter 3 "Hidden Danger"

Chapter 4 "The Tunnel of Terror"

Chapter 5 "The Black Dragon Strikes"

Chapter 6 "Flaming Havoc"

Chapter 7 "The Death Mist"

Chapter 8 "Satan Fires the Fuse"

Chapter 9 "Satanic Sabotage"

Chapter 10 "Trapped in a Blazing 'Chute'"

Chapter 11 "Undeclared War"

Chapter 12 "Civilian Courage Conquers"

Cast: Gene Reynolds, Lionel Atwill, Frank Albertson, Richard Lane, the Dead End Kids, Frankie Darro and David Gorcey

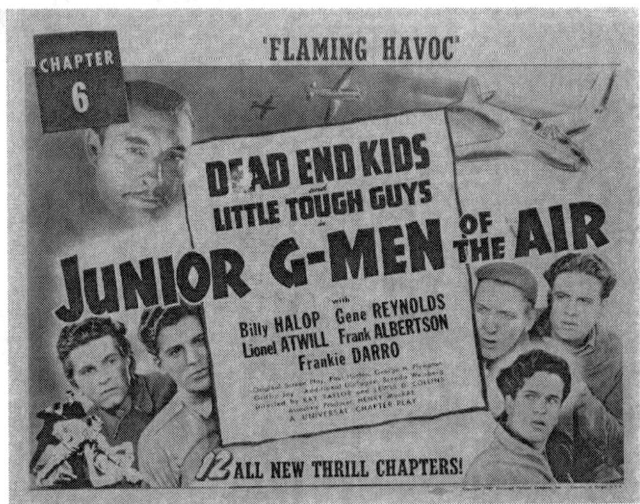

Chapter 4- poster for Jr. G-Men of the Air

Chapter-1 lobby card for Jr. G-Men of the Air-wings aflame

Jr. G-Men of the Air-chapter-6-lobby card

Tough As They Come

Universal Studios: Released June 5, 1942

Cast: Helen Parrish, Paul Kelly, Ann Gillis and the Dead End Kids

Title lobby card for the film Tough as They Come

Mob Town one sheet poster

Bernard Punsly shows off his boxing skills in this scene from Tough as They Come

Helen Parrish and Billy Halop in this publicity still for Tough as They Come

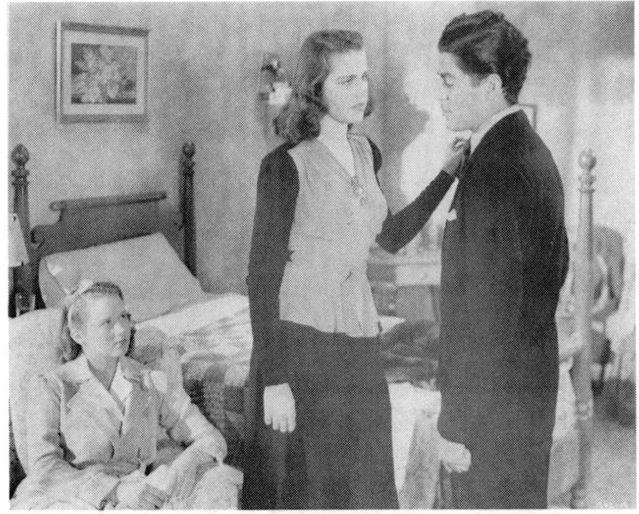

Scene from Tough as They Come

Billy Halop and Paul Kelly in a scene from Tough as They Come

Mug Town

Universal Studios: Released, January 22, 1943

<u>Cast</u>: Grace McDonald, Edward Norris, Paul Fix, Tommy Kelly, the Dead End Kids

Scene from Mug Town

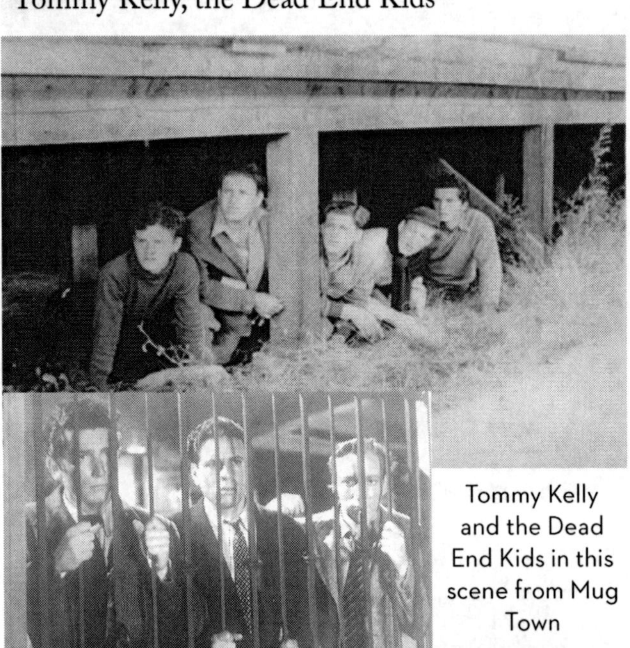

Tommy Kelly and the Dead End Kids in this scene from Mug Town

The kids are behind bars once again

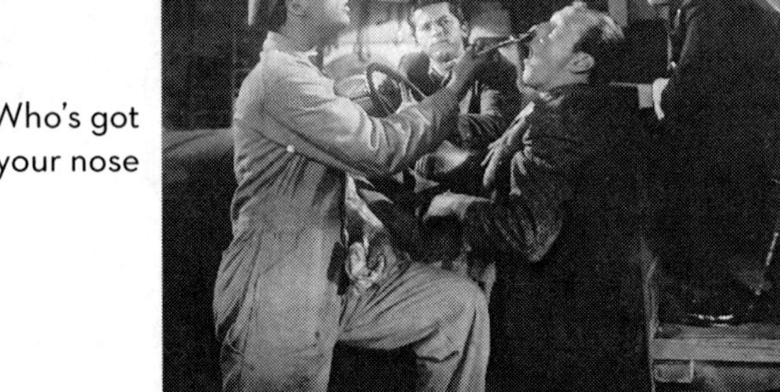

Who's got your nose

Gabe Dell,Huntz Hall and Billy Halop in a scene from the film Mug Town

Mug Town one sheet poster

Press photo for -Mug Town-with Dell-Hall and Halop

Keep'Em Slugging

Universal Studios: Released August 2, 1943

<u>Cast</u>: Evelyn Ankers, Elyse Knox, Don Porter, Shemp Howard, Milburn Stone, and as the Dead End Kids, Bobby Jordan, Gabe Dell, Huntz and Norman Abbott.

Lobby card for Keep'em Slugging

The kids in a scene from Keep'em Slugging

Scene still with Mary Gordan and Bobby Jordan

Scene still from Keep'em Slugging

Billy Halop and Paul Kelly in a scene from Tough as

Press book from Keep'em Slugging

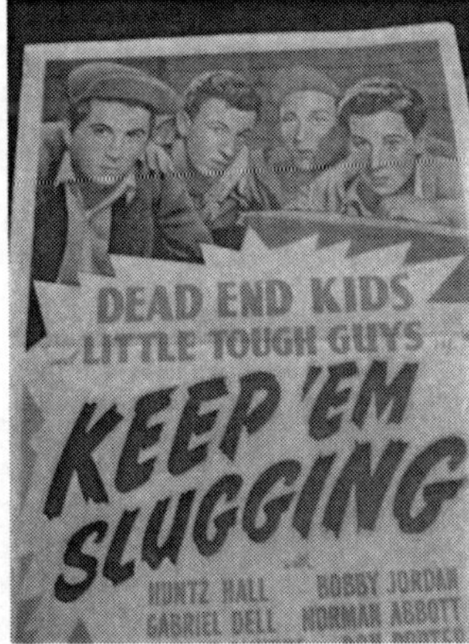

One sheet poster of the film Keep'em Slugging

Scene for Keep'em Slugging

Lobby card for Keep'em Slugging

Scene from Keep'em Slugging with Bobby Jordan

CHAPTER 4
The Little Tough Guy Films

Little Tough Guys in Society

Universal Studios: Released November 20, 1938

Cast: As The Little Tough Guys Charles R. Duncan, David Gorcey, Harris Berger, Billy Benedict, Hally Chester, Frankie Thomas, Lester Jay, and rounding out the cast, Mischa Auer, Mary Boland, Edward

Poster style c

Insert for Little Tough Guys in Society

The Little Tough Guys in Little Tough Guys in Society

Little Tough Guys in Society lobby card

Lobby Card from the film Little Tough Guys in Society

Jackie Searl and Mischa Auer in this publicity still from Little Tough Guys in Society

Little Tough Guys in Society one sheet poster

Little Tough Guys in Society poster, style b

Newsboys Home

Universal Studios: Released January 22, 1939

<u>Cast</u>: Jackie Cooper, Elisha Cook, Wendy Barrie, Edward Norris and as the Little Tough Guys Charles R. Duncan, David Gorcey, Hally Chester, Harris Berger, Billy Benedict.

6 stills from the film Newsboys Home

Boys Cimema magazine

Jackie Cooper and Elisha Cook Jr. square off in this scene from Newsboy's Home

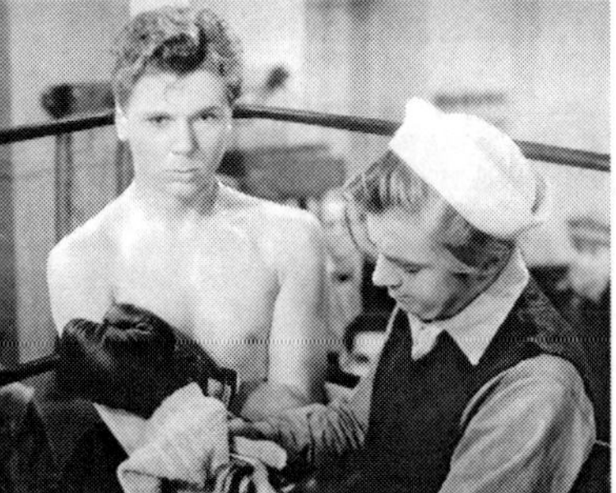

Jackie Cooper and Harris Berger in a scene from Newsboy's Home

Lobby card for Newsboys Home

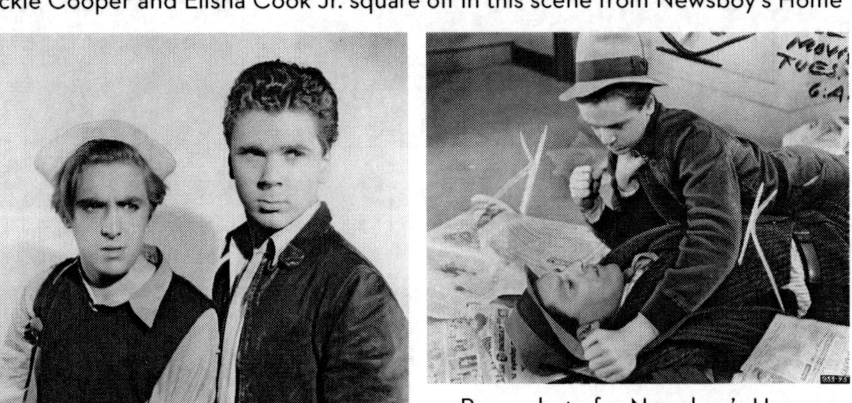

Harris Berger and Jackie Cooper Newsboy's Home

Press photo for Newsboy's Home

Jackie Cooper publicity still for the film Newsboy's Home

Code of the Streets

Universal Studios: Released April 17, 1939

Playing the parts of the Little Tough Guys Jimmy McCallion, Charles R. Duncan, Billy Benedict, David Gorcey, Harris Berger and Hally Chester, with Frankie Thomas, Harry Carey, Leon Ames, Marc Lawrence and Juanita Quigley.

Scene still from Code of the Streets

Scene from Code of the Streets

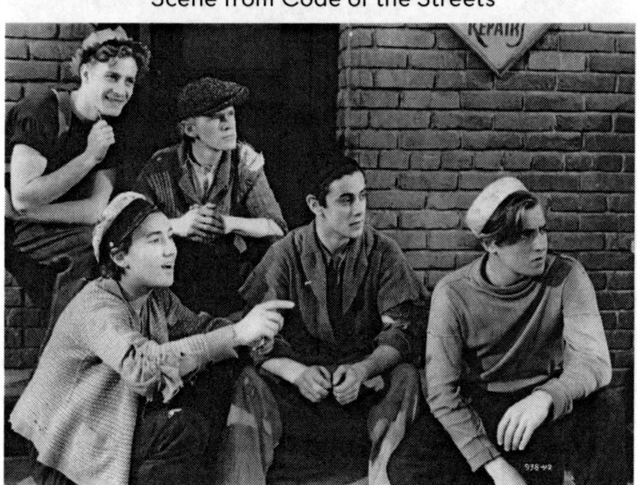

The Little Tough Guys

Code of the Streets-still

And you thought the Little Tough Guys couldnt sing

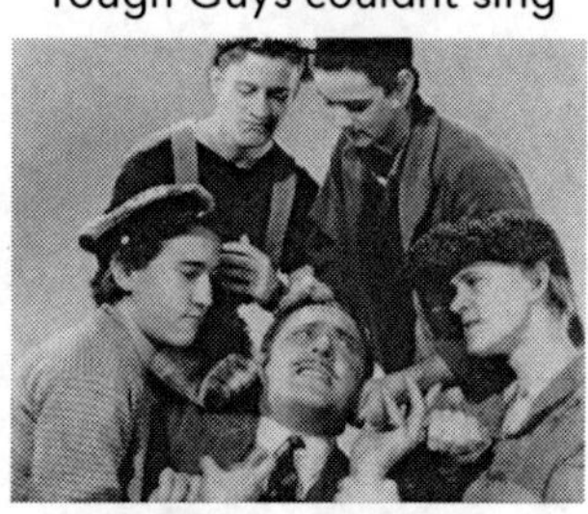

The little tough guys get the drop on Leon Ames

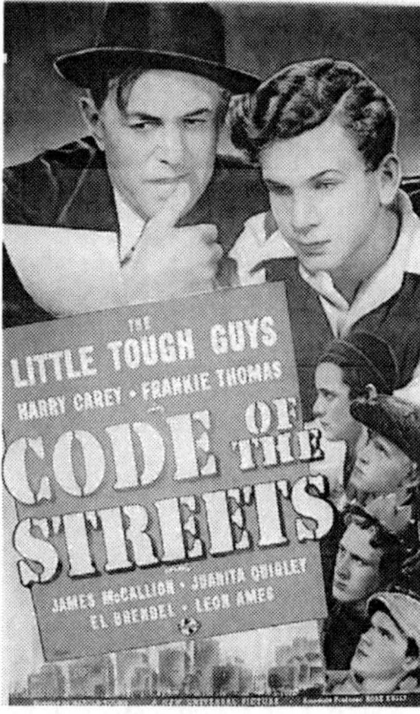

Poster for Code of the Streets

Code of the Streets with Frankie Thomas Charles-Duncan and Jimmy McCallion

Jimmy McCallion and Frankie Thomas publicity still

The Little Tough Guys in Code of the Streets

Boys Cinema magazine

CHAPTER 5
The East Side Kids Films — 1940-1945

In whole or in part, these were The East Side Kids

Leo Gorcey, Hally Chester, Bobby Jordan, Huntz Hall, Gabe Dell, Donald Haines, Frankie Burke, David Gorcey, Harris Berger, Eugene Francis, Dick Chandlee, Bobby Stone, Johnny Duncan, Sunshine Sammy Morrison, Buddy Gorman, Mendie Koenig, Bennie Bartlett, Stanley Clements, Billy Benedict, David Durand, Eddie Brain, Sam Edwards, Jimmy Strand, Jack Edwards, Bill Bates, Leo Borden, Eddie Mills, Al Stone and Bill Lawrence.

The East Side Kids years 1940-1945

East Side Kids

A Four Bell Production/Released by Monogram Pictures on February 10, 1940

Cast: Starring the Original East Side Kids, Donald Haines, Sam Edwards, Harris Berger, Jack Edwards, Eddie Brain and Frankie Burke. With Leon Ames, Dennis Moore, Joyce Bryant, Dave O'Brien and Vince Barnett.

Dave O'Brien and Harris Berger square off in this scene from the East Side Kids

Scene from the film The East Side Kids

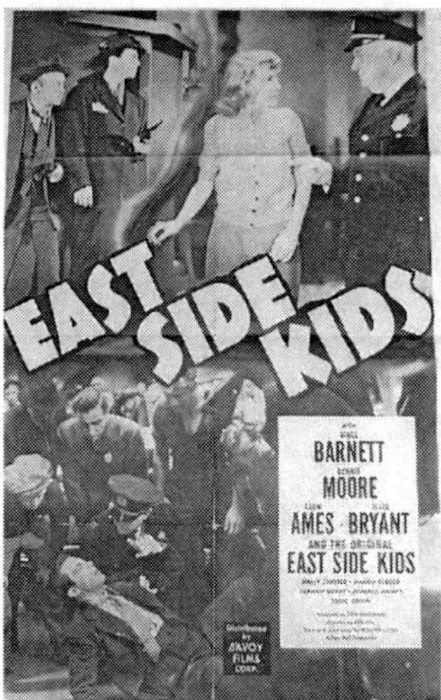

East Side kids One Sheet Poster

The Original East Side Kids

Boys of the City

A Four Bell Production/Released by Monogram Pictures on July 15, 1940

Cast: Bobby Jordan, Leo Gorcey, Donald Haines, Hally Chester, Frankie Burke, Sunshine Sammy Morrison, and Eugene Francis, Dave O'Brien and Dennis Moore.

Notes: After the release of *East Side Kids*, Frankie Burke was in only one other film as an East Side Kid, *Boys of the City*. Hally Chester would take part in one other feature; Harris Berger, Sam Edwards and brother Jack were dropped. Taking over the helm as the East Side Kids were the following: Bobby Jordan, Leo Gorcey, Johnny Duncan, Dick Chandlee, Eddie Mills, Billy Benedict, David Gorcey, Mendie Koenig, Donald Haines, Eugene Francis, Bill Lawrence, Jimmy Strand, Buddy Gorman and Bennie Bartlett.

Boys of the City lobby card

Press book for Boys of City

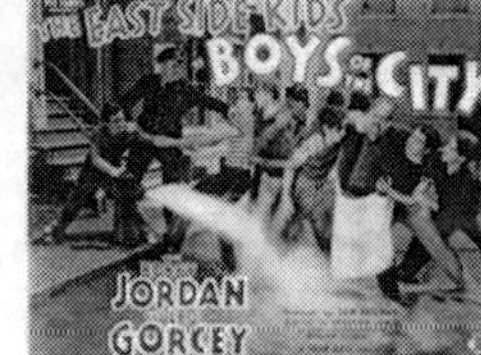

Lobby card for Boys of the City

One sheet poster-Boys of the City

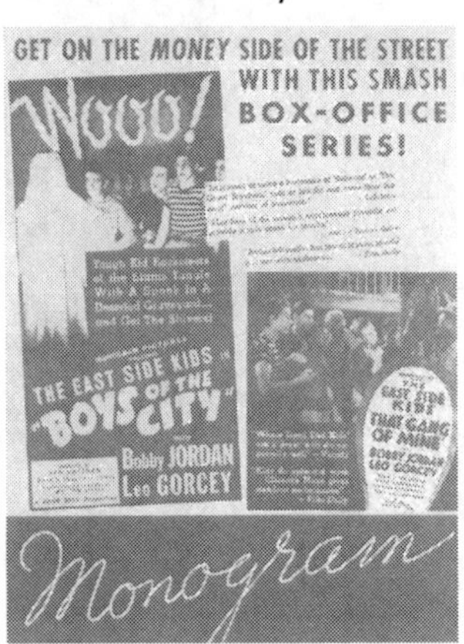

Monogram picture's flyer

Scene still for Boys of the City

That Gang of Mine

A Four Bell Production/Released by Monogram Pictures on September 23, 1940

Cast: The East Side Kids with Eugene Francis, Clarence Muse and Milton Kibbee.

Lobby Card for That Gang of Mine

Scene still from That Gang of Mine

Scene from the film That Gang of Mine

That Gang of Mine lobby card

Pride of the Bowery

A Banner Production/Released by Monogram Pictures on January 24, 1941

Cast: The East Side Kids/added to the East Side Kids as members are David Gorcey, Bobby Stone, with Kenneth Howell, Carleton Young and Mary Ainsley.

Lobby card from Pride of the Bowery

Lobby card from Pride of the Bowery

Lobby card for the film Pride of the Bowery

Pride of the Bowery lobby card

Flying Wild

A Banner Production/Released by Monogram Pictures on April 11, 1941

Cast: The East Side Kids, with Joan Barclay, Forrest Taylor and Dennis Moore.

Notes: Eugene Francis left the series for the Military.

The EAST SIDE KIDS...
"FLYING WILD"

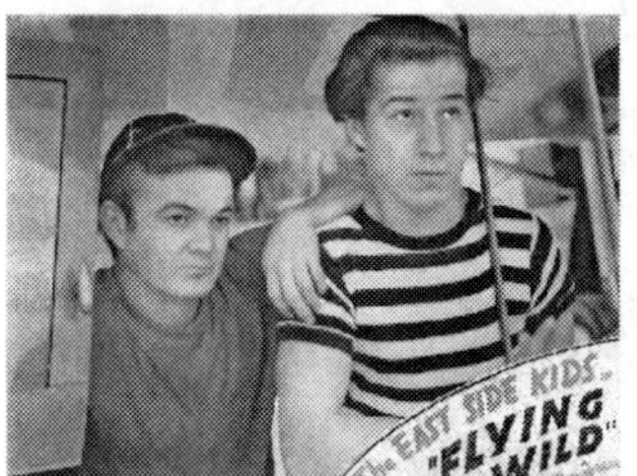

Mint-lobby card for the film Flying Wild

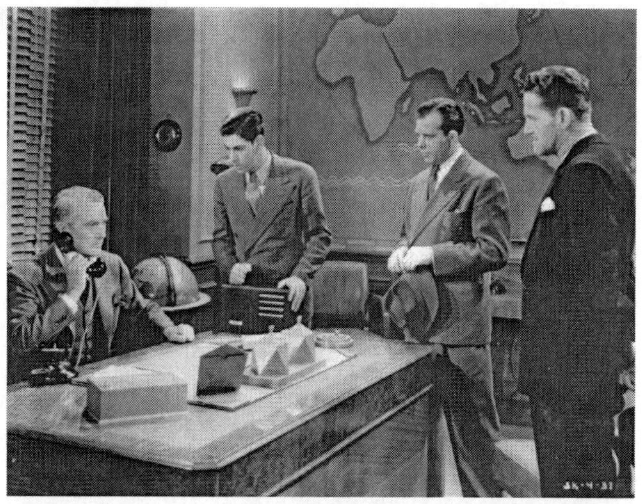

Scene from Flying Wild,Eugene Francis tries to make his point

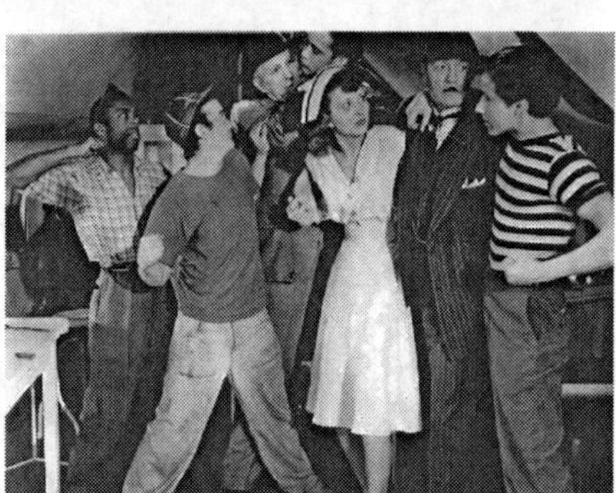

Lobby card from Pride of the Bowery

The EAST SIDE KIDS...
"FLYING WILD"

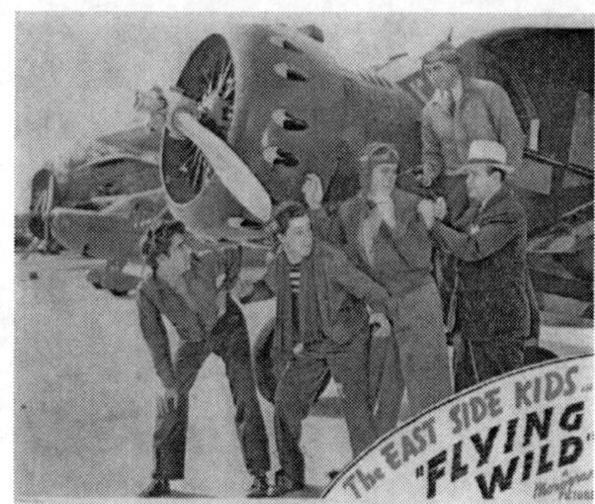

Lobby Card for the film Flying Wild

The
EAST SIDE KIDS IN
"FLYING WILD"
WITH
LEO GORCEY ★ BOBBY JORDAN
Produced by SAM KATZMAN
Directed by WILLIAM WEST · Story and Screenplay by AL MARTIN
A BANNER PICTURES Production
Distributed by SAVOY FILMS CORP.

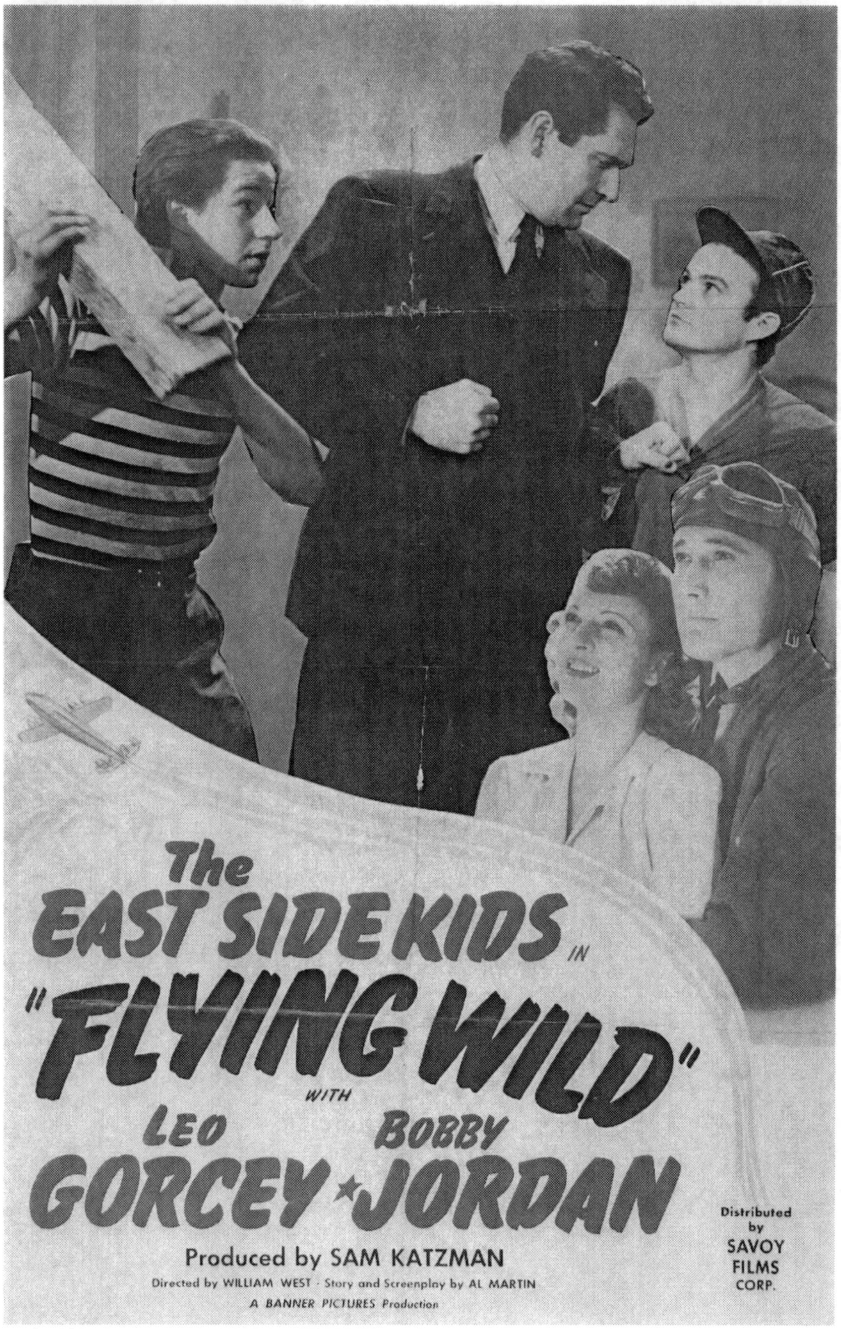

Poster of the film Flying Wild

Bowery Blitzkrieg

A Banner Production/Released by Monogram Pictures on September 8, 1941

Cast: The East Side Kids, added to the cast is Keye Luke, Warren Hull, Charlotte Henry and Jack Mulhall.

Notes: Added to the cast as an East Side Kid is Huntz Hall.

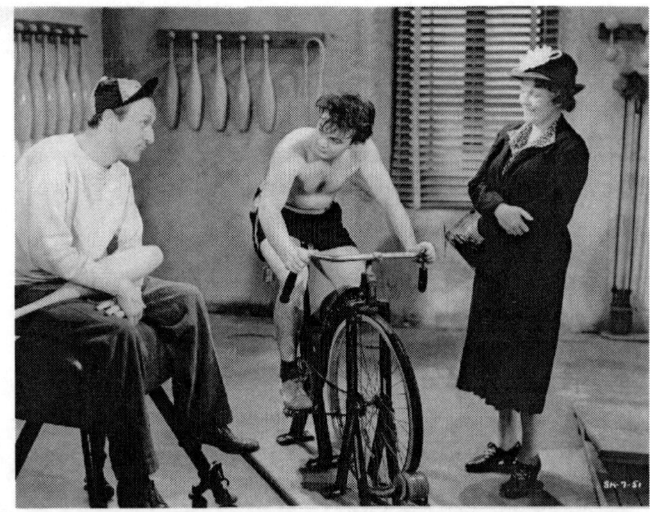

Press photo-Bowery Blitzkrieg

Scene from Bowery Blitzkrieg

Poster for Bowery Blitzkrieg

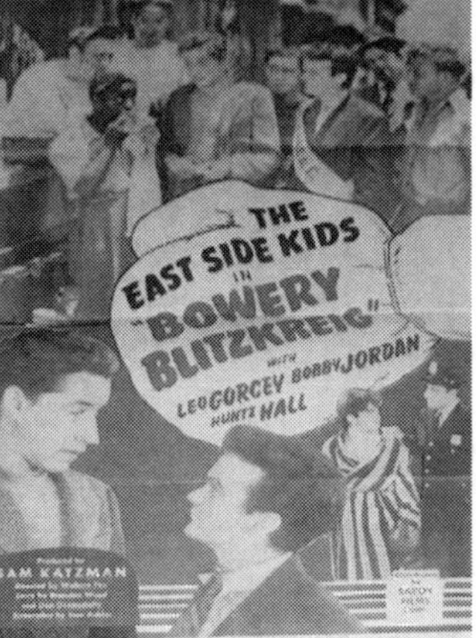

One Sheet Poster for Bowery Blitzkrieg

Bobby Stone and Bobby Jordan in this lobby card

Lobby card for Bowery Blitzkrieg

Spooks Run Wild

A Banner Production/Released by Monogram Pictures on October 24, 1941

Cast: The East Side Kids, along with Bela Lugosi, Angelo Rossitto and Dave O'Brien.

Notes: Soon after the release of this film, Donald Haines enlisted in the Military

Black in white scene still -just like lobby card

Lobby Card of the film Spooks Run Wild

Scene from the film Spooks Run Wild

Lobby Card-Bela does his magic

Dave O'Brian has the upper hand

Lobby Card for Spooks Run Wild

Spooks Run Wild-poster-1941 reissue

Mr. Wise Guy

A Banner Production/Released by Monogram Pictures on February 20, 1942

Cast: The East Side Kids, Billy Gilbert, Guinn (Big Boy) Williams, Joan Barclay, Ann Doran and Douglas Fowley

Notes: Gabriel Dell makes his first appearance with the kids. William (Bill) Lawrence playing the part of Skinny, makes his only contribution in this film, and is never heard from again.

Billy Gilbert, Sidney Miller and the East Side Kids in this scene from Mr. Wise Guy

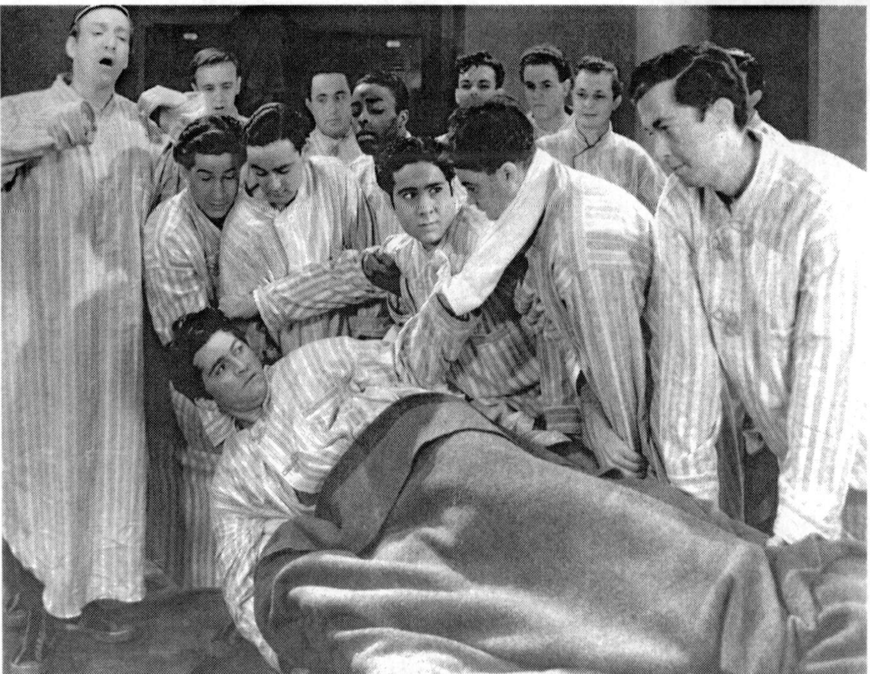

Bill Lawrence in his only shot at fame-far right

Scene from Mr. Wise Guy

Scene still from the film Mr. Wise Guy

The East Side Kids in this scene from Mr. Wise Guy

Scene for Mr. Wise Guy

Let's Get Tough

A Banner Production/Released by Monogram Pictures on May 22, 1942

Cast: The East Side Kids, Gabriel Dell, Robert Armstrong, Phil Ahn, Florence Rice and Tom Brown.

Theater program

Lets Get Tough poster from belgin

Let's Get Tough-lobby card

Lobby card from the film Let's Get Tough

Lobby card

Scene for the film Lets Get Tough

Smart Alecks

A Banner Production/Released by Monogram Pictures on August 7, 1942

Cast: The East Side Kids, Gabriel Dell, Gale Storm, Slappy Maxie Rosenbloom, Roger Pryor, Walter Woolf King, Sam Bernard and Stanley Clememts.

Notes: David Gorcey left the series for military duty; enter Stanley Clements as one of the gang.

Scene from Smart Aleck's

Lobby card for the film Smart Aleck's

Press book for Smart Aleck's

Kid Dynamite

A Banner Production/Released by Monogram Pictures on February 12, 1943

Cast: The East Side Kids, Gabriel Dell, Pamela Blake, Vince Barnett and Minerva Urecal.

Notes: Bennie Bartlett and David Durand make their first appearance as East Side Kids.

Bobby Jordan and Noah Berry, Jr.

Neath Brooklyn Bridge lobby card

One sheet poster for Neath Brooklyn Bridge

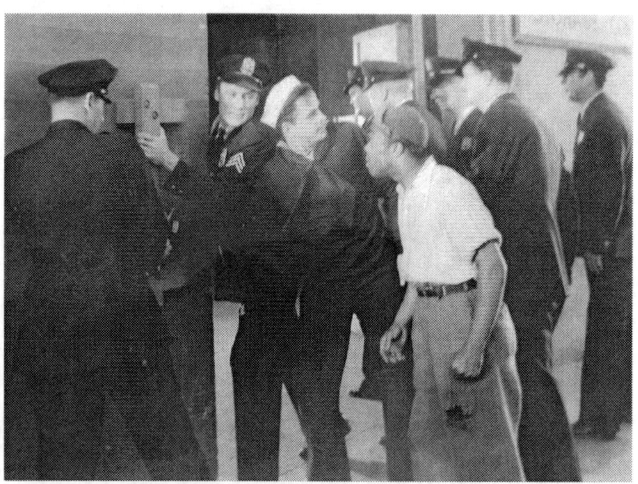

Scene from Neath Brooklyn Bridge

Noah Beery,Jr. and Anne Gills in a publicity still from Neath Brooklyn Bridge

Kid Dynamite

A Banner Production/Released by Monogram Pictures on February 12, 1943

Cast: The East Side Kids, Gabriel Dell, Pamela Blake, Vince Barnett and Minerva Urecal.

Notes: Bennie Bartlett and David Durand make their first appearance as East Side Kids.,

Kid Dynamite-lobby card

Lobby card from Kid Dynamite

One Sheet Poster for the film Kid Dynamite

Clancy Street Boys

A Banner Production, Released by Monogram Pictures on April 27, 1943

<u>Cast</u>: The East Side Kids, Dick Chandlee and Eddie Mills (who make their only appearance as part of the east side gang), Noah Berry Sr., Amelita

Clancy Street lobby card

Eddie Mills, Dick Chandlee in there only film as East Side Kids

Poster of Clancy Street Boys

Ghosts on the Loose

A Banner Production, Released by Monogram Pictures on July 30, 1943

Cast: The East Side Kids, Ava Gardner, Bela Lugosi, Ric Vallin and Bill Bates

Notes: Sammy Morrison ends his run as an East Side Kid, entering the Military

Lobby Card from Ghosts on the Loose

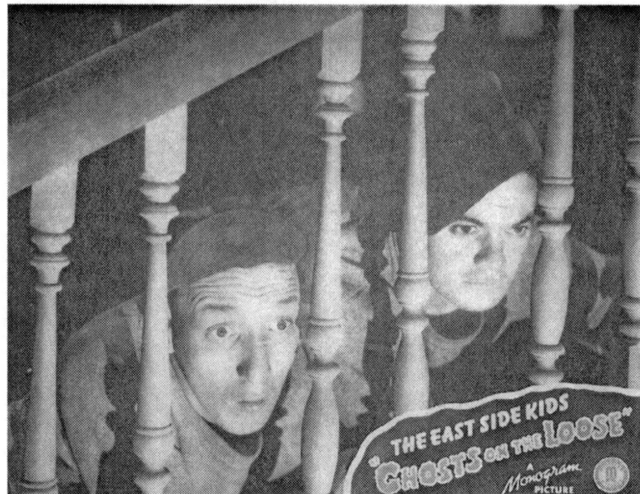

Huntz Hall and Leo Gorcey in this lobby card from Ghosts on the Loose

Scene from Ghosts on the Loose with Leo Gorcey and Huntz Hall

Sammy Morrison in this lobby card for the film Ghosts on the Loose

Ghosts on the Loose lobby card

Mr. Muggs Steps Out

A Banner Production, Released by Monogram Pictures on October 29, 1943

Cast: The East Side Kids, Nick Stuart, Joan Marsh and Kay Marvis.

Notes: Jimmy Strand becomes an East Side Kid, while Kay Marvis weds Leo Gorcey.

Lobby Card from the film Mr. Muggs Steps Out

Mr. Muggs Steps Out poster

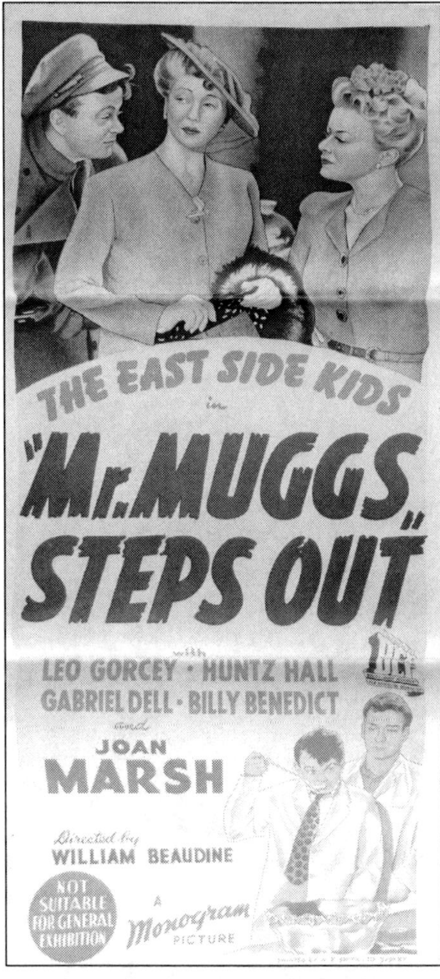

Insert for Mr. Muggs Steps Out

Million Dollar Kid

A Banner Production, Released by Monogram Pictures on February 28, 1944

Cast: The East Side Kids, Johnny Duncan, Herbert Heyes, Louise Currie, Iris Adrian and Al Stone.

Notes: Buddy Gorman and Johnny Duncan join the gang, while Al Stone is a one trick pony.

Million Dollar Kid scene still

Whats on your mind

Leo Gorcey, Jimmy Strand, Buddy Gorman, David Durand and Huntz Hall in a scene from Million Dollar Kid

Scene from Million Dollar Kid

Million Dollar Kid scene

Follow the Leader

A Banner Production, Released by Monogram Pictures on June 3, 1944

Cast: The East Side Kids, Joan Marsh, Jack La Rue, Bernard Gorcey and the Sherill Sisters with Gene Austin.

Notes: David Durand and Bobby Stone leave the series, joining the service.

Scene from Follow the Leader

Poster for Follow the Leader

David Durand and Billy Benedict in a scene from Follow the Leader

Follow the Leader lobby card

Block Busters

A Banner Production, Released be Monogram Pictures on July 22, 1944

<u>Cast</u>: The East Side Kids, Bernard Gorcey, Bill Channey, Fredrick Pressel, Kay Gorcey, Minerva Urecal, with Jimmie Noon and his Orchestra featuring The Ashburns.

Block Busters Lobby Card

Poster for Block Busters

Bowery Champs

A Banner Production, Released by Monogram Pictures on November 25, 1944

<u>Cast</u>: The East Side Kids, Thelma White, Bobby Jordan, Bernard Gorcey and Evelyn Brent.

<u>Notes</u>: Bobby Jordan was on leave from the service for his part in this film

Scene from Bowery Champs

Bowery Champs scene

Lobby card Bowery Champs

Docks of New York

A Banner Production, Released by Monogram Pictures on February 24, 1945

Cast: The East Side Kids, Mendie Koenig, Carlyle Blackwell, Cy Kendall, Gloria Pope, Bernard Gorcey and Leo Borden.

Notes: Mendie Koenig makes his debut. Leo Borden's playing the part of Peter was his only chance at stardom. It didn't pan out, and he's been forgotten.

Lobby card for the film Docks of New York

Docks of New York-color still-only one I have ever seen

Lobby Card for Docks of New york

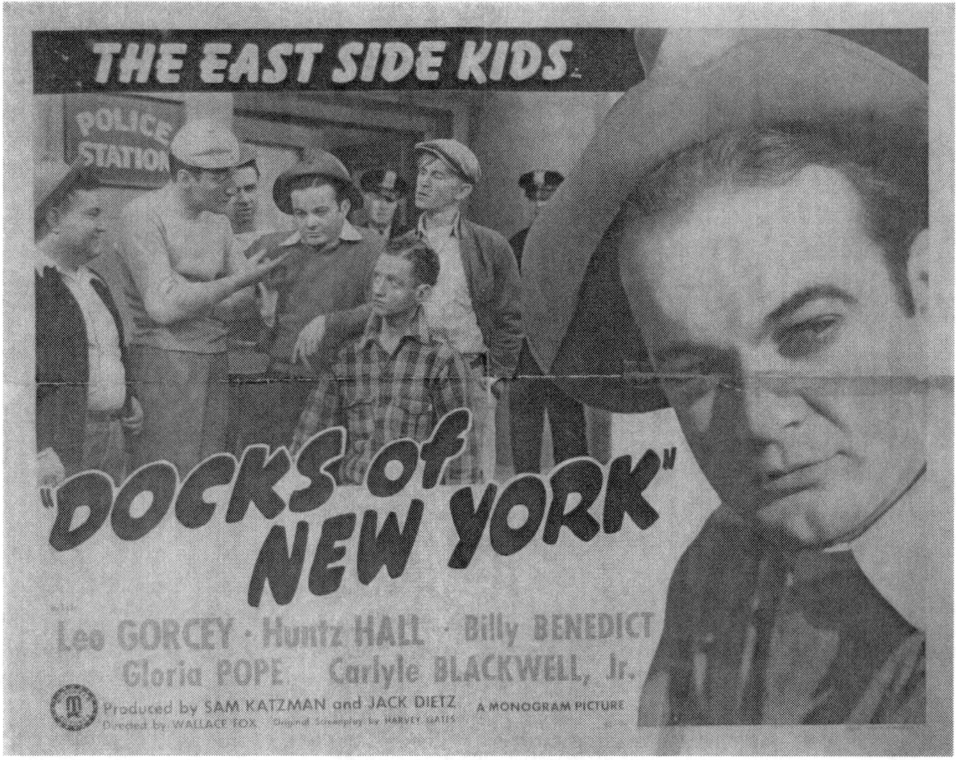

Lobby Card for Docks of New York

Lobby Card from the film Docks of New York

Mr. Muggs Rides Again

A Banner Production, Released by Monogram Pictures on July 15, 1945

Cast: The East Side Kids, Nancy Brinckman, John H. Allen and George Meeker.

Lobby card for Mr. Muggs Rides Again

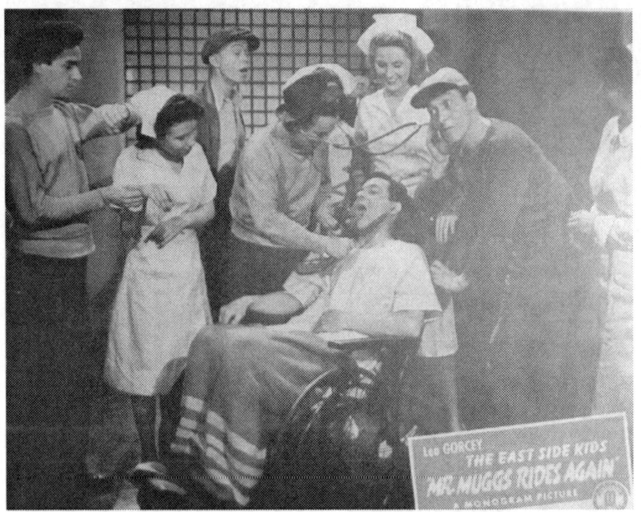

Lobby card from Mr. Muggs Rides Again

Scene from Mr. Muggs Rides Again

Come Out Fighting

A Banner Production, Released by Monogram Pictures on September 29, 1945

Cast: The East Side Kids , Leo Gorcey, Huntz Hall, Billy Benedict, Mendie Koenig, Buddy Gorman,

Lobby Card for the film Come Out Fighting

Scene from Come Out Fighting-they sure do

MONOGRAM PICTURES presents

LEO GORCEY

AND

THE EAST SIDE KIDS

IN

"COME OUT FIGHTING"

with HUNTZ HALL · BILLY BENEDICT

GABRIEL DELL

Produced by SAM KATZMAN and JACK DIETZ

Directed by William Beaudine

Story and Screenplay by Earl Snell

Lobby card from the film Come Out Fighting

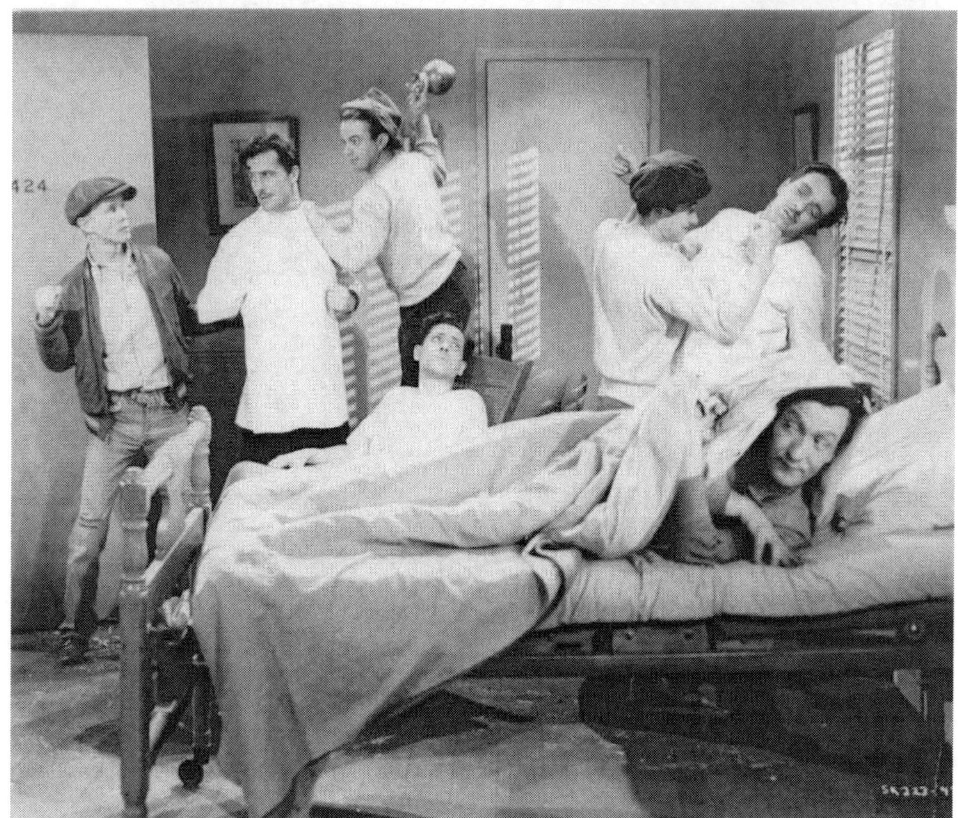

The East Side Kids in Come Out Fighting

Buddy Gorman and Mendie Koenig in a scene for the film Come Out Fighting

Scene for the film Come Out Fighting

CHAPTER 6
The Bowery Boys Films – 1946-1958

These were The Bowery Boys:

Leo Gorcey, Bobby Jordan, Gabe Dell, Huntz Hall, Billy Benedict, David Gorcey, Stanley Clements, Buddy Gorman, Gil Straton Jr., Bennie Bartlett, William Frambes, Eddie Leroy, Bernard Gorcey and Jimmy Murphy.

Live Wires

Monogram: Released January 12, 1946

Cast: The Bowery Boys, Pamela Blake, Mike Mazurki, Patti Brill, John Eldrige and Claudia Drake.

Poster for the film Live Wires

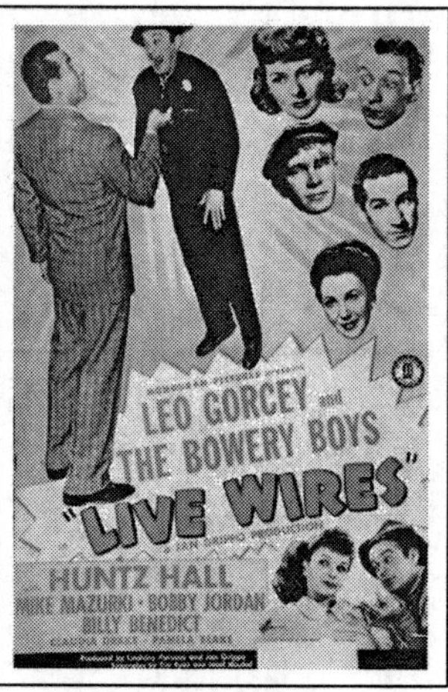

One sheet poster for Live Wires

Patta Brill is all ears in this scene from Live Wires

Mike Mazurki has a hold of Slip in this scene from Live Wires

Live Wires lobby card

Scene still from Live Wires

Scene from the film Live Wires

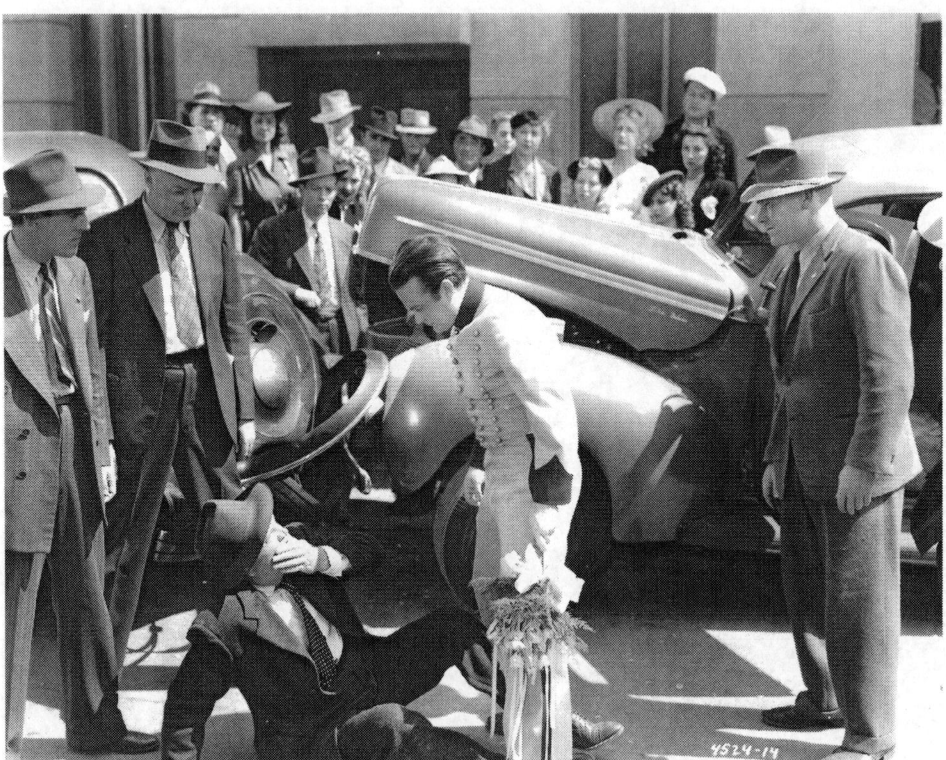

Scene from Live Wires

In Fast Company

Monogram: Released June 20, 1946

<u>Cast</u>: The Bowery Boys, Judy Clark, Charles D. Brown, Jane Randolph, Paul Harvey, Mary Gordan and Douglas Fowley.

One sheet Poster

Scene for the film In Fast Company

Scene from the film In Fast Company

In Fast Company-lobby card with George-Eldredge and Leo Gorcey

Slip turns on the charm in this still from In Fast Company

Half Sheet Poster

Scene from In Fast Company

Bowery Bombshell

Monogram: Released July 20, 1946

<u>Cast</u>: The Bowery Boys, Teala Loring, James Burke, Sheldon Leonard, William "Wee Willie" Davis and Vince Barnett.

Bowery Bombshell lobby card

Lobby card from the film Bowery Bombshell

One sheet poster

Lobby card for Bowery Bombshell

Spook Busters

Monogram: Released August 24, 1946

<u>Cast</u>: The Bowery Boys, Douglass Dumbrille, Tanis Chandler, Charles Middleton, Maurice Cass, Richard Alexander and Chester Clute.

Scene from Spook Busters

Scene for Spook Busters

Spook Busters scene

Lobby card for Spook Busters

Douglass Dumbrille,Huntz Hall and Leo Gorcey in this scene from Spook Busters

Spook Busters one sheet poster

Mr. Hex

Monogram: Released December 7, 1946

Cast: The Bowery Boys, Ben Welden, Gale Robbins, Sammy Cohen, Danny Beck and Eddie Gribbon.

Cap-lobby card from Mr. Hex

Lobby card for the film Mr. Hex

Scene from the film Mr. Hex

Mr. Hex half sheet poster

Mr. Hex lobby card

Mr. Hex one sheet poster

Lobby card for Mr. Hex

Still from Mr. Hex

Poster for Mr. Hex

Hard Boiled Mahoney

Monogram: Released April 26, 1947

Cast: The Bowery Boys, Dan Seymour, Teala Loring, Betty Compson, Danny Beck, Byron Foulger and Pierre Watkin.

Scene still from Hard Boild Mahoney

Teala Loring,Dan Seymour and the Bowery Boys in this scene

One sheet poster

Leo Gorcey and Byron Foulger share a scene from Hard Boiled Mahoney

Lobby card for Hard Boiled Mahoney

Scene from Hard Boiled Mahoney

News Hounds

Monogram: Released August 13, 1947

Cast: The Bowery Boys, Tim Ryan, Bill Kennedy, Christine McIntyre, Anthony Caruso, Ralph Dunn, John Elliott and John Alexander.

The Bowery Boys in a scene from News Hounds

News Hounds insert

Anthony Caruso,Leo Gorcey and Christine McIntyre in this publicity still from News Hounds

Scene from News Hounds

Lobby card for News Hounds

NEWS HOUNDS large

Bowery Buckaroos

Monogram: Released November 22, 1947

<u>Cast</u>: The Bowery Boys, Julie Gibson, Jack Norman, Iron Eyes Cody, Minerva Urecal, Russell Simpson and Rosa Turich.

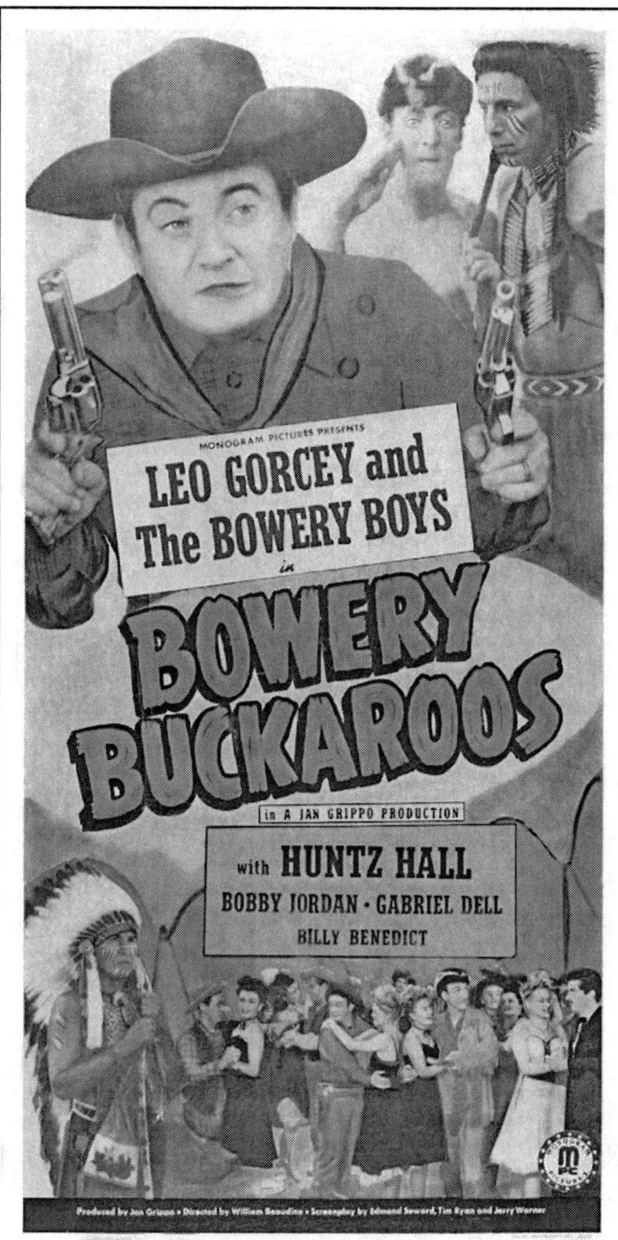

Bowery Buckaroos insert poster

Scene still from Bowery Buckaroos

Scene from Bowery Buckaroos

Publicity still from the film Bowery Buckaroos

Bowery Buckaroos lobby card

Angels' Alley

Monogram: Released March 21, 1948

Cast: The Bowery Boys, Frankie Darro, Nestor Paiva, Rosemary La Planche, Nelson Leigh, Tommie Menzies, Mary Gordon and John Eldredge.

Leo Gorcey and Rosemary LaPlanche in this publicity still for Angel's Alley

One sheet poster for Angel's Alley

Publicity still from Angel's Alley

Lobby card for Angel's Alley

Title lobby card for Angel's Alley

Jinx Money

Monogram: Released June 27, 1948

Cast: The Bowery Boys, Sheldon Leonard, Donald MacBride, Ben Welden, John Eldredge, Betty Caldwell, Lucien Littefeld and Ralph Dunn.

Jinx Money lobby card

Poster for Jinx Money

Jinx Money press book

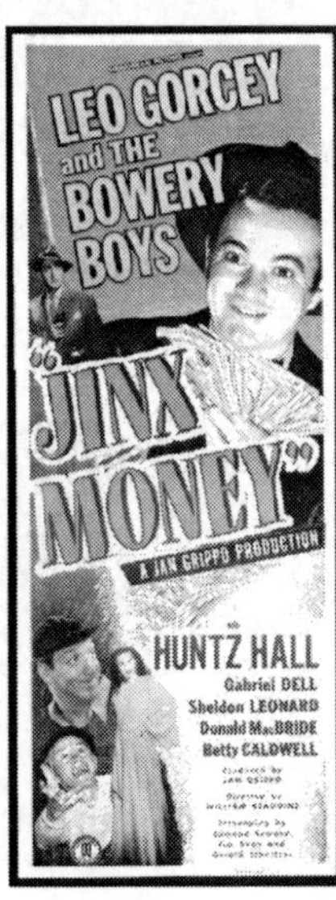

Insert for Jinx Money

Smuggler's Cove

Monogram: Released October 24, 1948

Cast: The Bowery Boys, Paul Harvey, Martin Kosleck, Amelita Ward, Eddie Gribbon and Jaqueline Dalya.

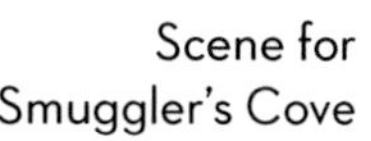
Scene for Smuggler's Cove

Lobby card for Smuggler's Cove

Lobby card for Smuggler's Cove

Smuggler's Cove lobby card

Trouble Makers

Monogram: Released December 10, 1948

Cast: The Bowery Boys, Fritz Feld, Helen Parrish, Frankie Darro, John Ridgely, Lionel Stander, Cliff Clark and William Ruhl.

Lobby card for Trouble Makers

Scene from Trouble Makers

Insert for Trouble Makers

Trouble Makers 3 Sheet poster

Fighting Fools

Monogram: Released April 17, 1949

Cast: The Bowery Boys, Ben Weldon, Frankie Darro, Lyle Talbot, Tom Kennedy, Evelyn Eaton, Dorothy Vaughan, Teddy Infuhr and Frank Moran.

Fighting Fools lobby card

Lobby card from Fighting Fools

Fighting Fools-Bert Conway and Frankie Darro in this scene

Scene from Fighting Fools

Insert from Fighting Fools

Hold That Baby

Monogram: Released June 26, 1949

Cast: The Bowery Boys, John Kellogg, Max Marx, Anabel Shaw and Frankie Darro.

Scene from Hold That Baby

One sheet poster for Hold That Baby

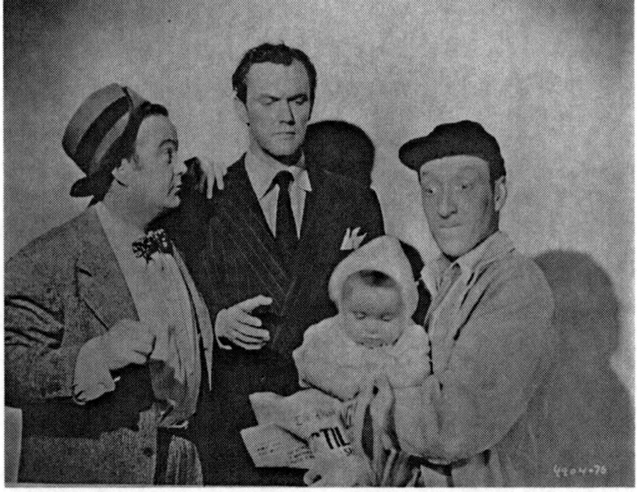

Leo Gorcey, John Kellogg and Huntz Hall in this publicity still from Hold That Baby

Angels in Disguise

Monogram: Released September 11, 1949

Cast: The Bowery Boys, Pepe Hern, Joe Turkel, Mickey Knox, Richard Benedict, Edward Ryan, Jean Dean, Rory Mallinson, Ray Walker and Marie Blake.

Publicity still with Edward Ryan and Leo Gorcey from Angels in Disguise

LEO GORCEY and the Bowery Boys
"Angels in Disguise"
HUNTZ HALL

Lobby card for the film Angels in Disguise

Scene from the film Angels in Disguise

One sheet poster for the film Angels in Disguise

Insert from Angles in Disguise

Master Minds

Monogram: Released November 20, 1949

Cast: The Bowery Boys, Glenn Strange, Alan Napier, William Yetter, Jane Adams and Skelton Knaggs.

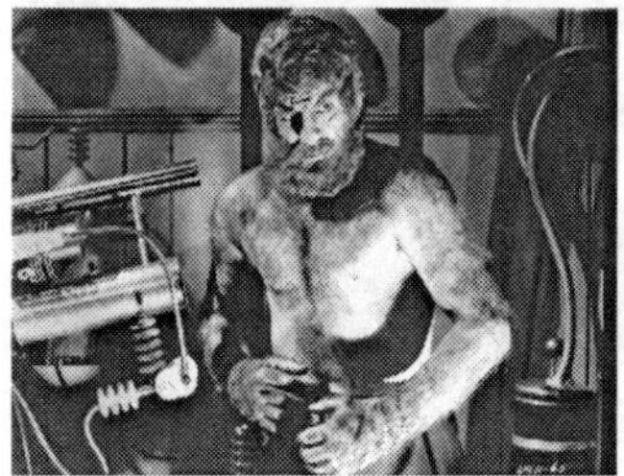

Genn Strange as Atlas in Master Minds

Scene from Master Minds

Lobby card for the film Master Minds

Master Minds one sheet poster

Blonde Dynamite

Monogram: Released February 12, 1950

<u>Cast</u>: The Bowery Boys, Adele Jergens, Lynn Davies, Beverlee Crane, Karen Randle, Jody Gilbert and John Harmon.

Scene from Blonde Dynamite, autographed by Buddy Gorman

Lobby card for Blonde Dynamite

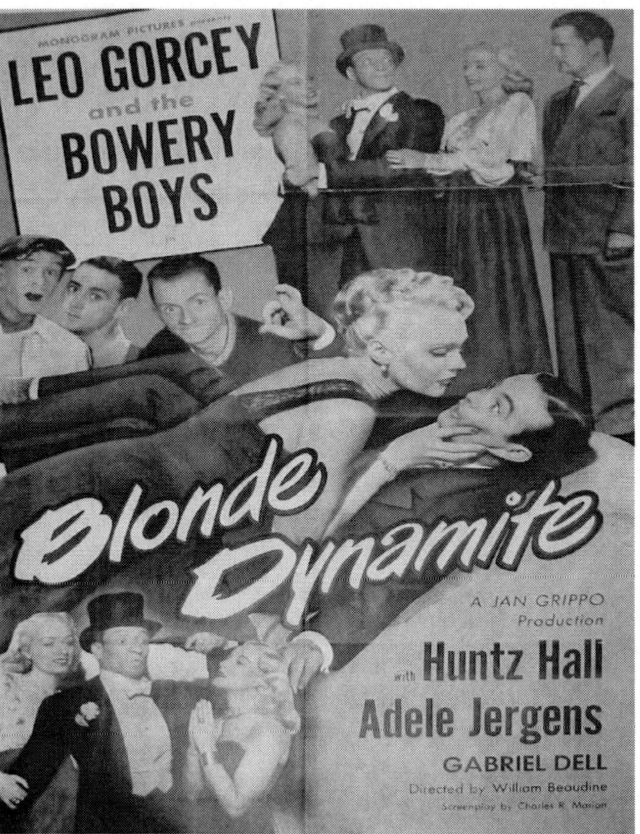

One sheet poster for Blonde Dynamite

Lucky Losers

Monogram: Released May14, 1950

<u>Cast</u>: The Bowery Boys, Lyle Talbot, Hillary Brooke, Joe Turkel, Harry Tyler and Frank Jenks.

Lucky Losers Poster

Insert for Lucky Losers

Lucky Losers scene still

Lobby card for Lucky Losers

Triple Trouble

Monogram: Released August 13, 1950

Cast: The Bowery Boys, Richard Benedict, Pat Collins, George Chandler, Paul Dubov and Joe Turkel.

Lobby card from Triple Trouble

Staged scene for the film Triple Trouble

Insert for Triple Trouble

Lobby card for Triple Trouble Lucky Losers Poster

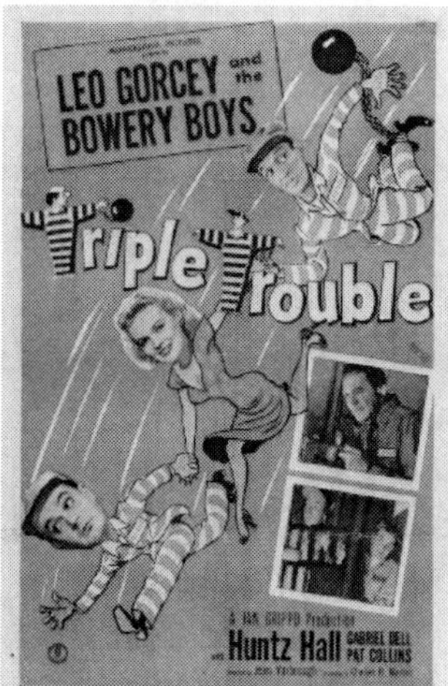

Triple Trouble one sheet poster

Scene from Triple Trouble

Blues Busters

Monogram: Released October 29, 1950

Cast: The Bowery Boys, Craig Stevens, Adele Jergens, Phillis Coates and William Vincent.

Blues Busters lobby card

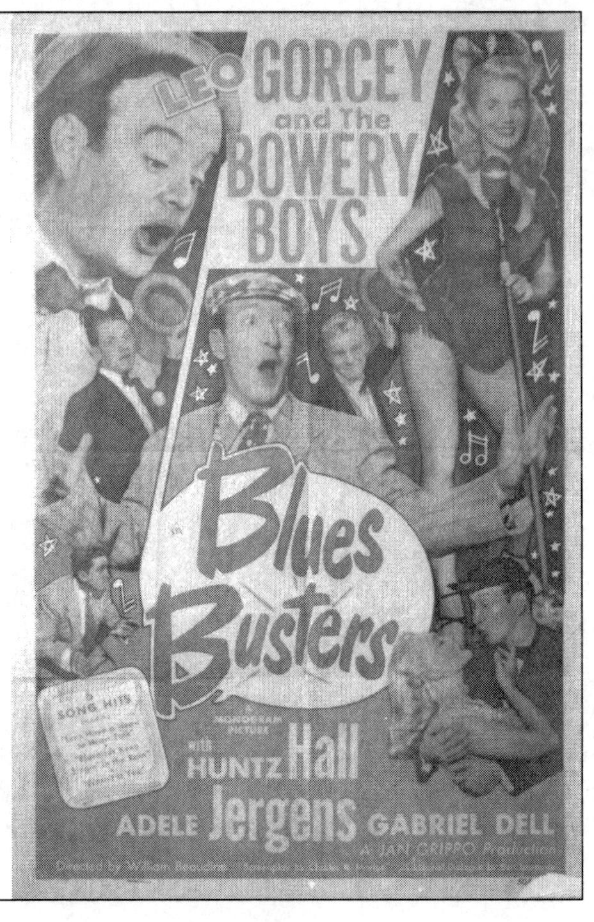

One sheet poster for Blues Busters

Lobby card from Blues Busters

Bowery Battalion

Monogram: Released January 24, 1951

<u>Cast</u>: The Bowery Boys, Donald MacBride, Virginia Hewitt, Russel Hicks, Harry Lauter and Emil Sitka.

Publicity still from Bowery Battalion

Bowery Battalion scene

Bowery Battalion poster

Scene from Bowery Battalion

Lobby card for Bowery Battalion

Ghost Chasers

Monogram: Released April 29, 1951

Cast: The Bowery Boys, Jan Kayne, Philip Van Zandt, Robert Coogan, Lloyd Corrigan and Donald Lawton.

Lobby card for Ghosts Chasers

Ghost Chasers lobby card

4 lobby cards from the film Ghost Chasers

Let's Go Navy!

Monogram: Released July 29, 1951

Cast: The Bowery Boys, Allen Jenkins, Richard Benedict, Tom Neal, George Offerman, Charlita, Paul Harvey, Dorothy Ford and Frank Jenks.

Lobby card for Let's Go Navy!

Scene from Let's Go Navy!

A very rare one sheet poster for the film Let's Go Navy-(notice working title for the film) makes this poster extremely rare!

Scene still from Let's Go Navy!

Insert for Let's Go Navy!

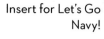

Crazy Over Horses

Monogram: Released November 21, 1951

Cast: The Bowery Boys, Ted de Corsia, Mike Ross, Tim Ryan, Gloria Saunders, Peggy Wynne, Perc Launders and Allen Jenkins.

Lobby card for Crazy Over Horses

Lobby card for Crazy Over Horses

Crazy Over Horses insert poster

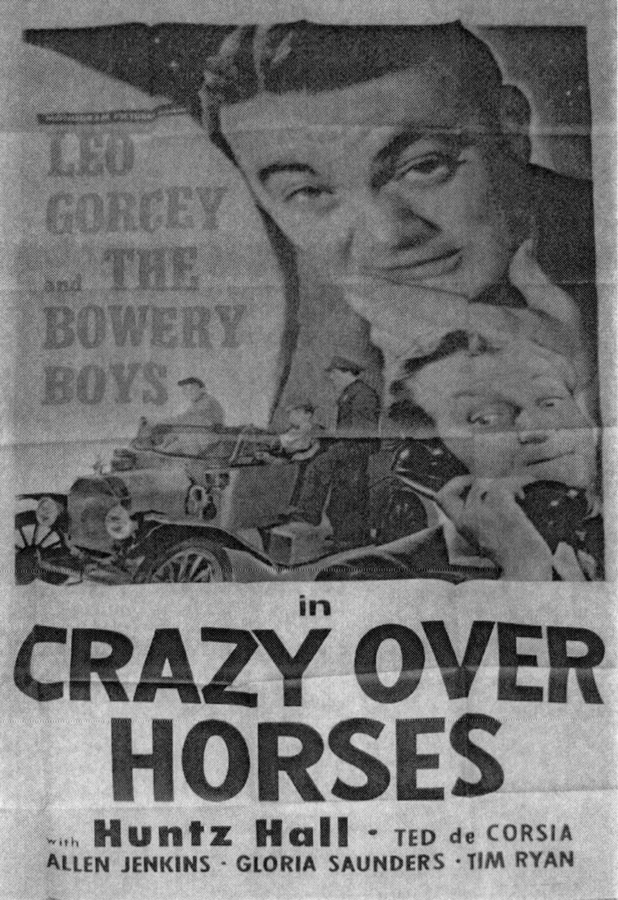

Six sheet poster for Crazy Over Horses

Hold That Line

Monogram: Released March 23, 1952

Cast: The Bowery Boys, John Bromfield, Taylor Holmes, Mona Knox, Francis Pierlot and Pierre Watkin.

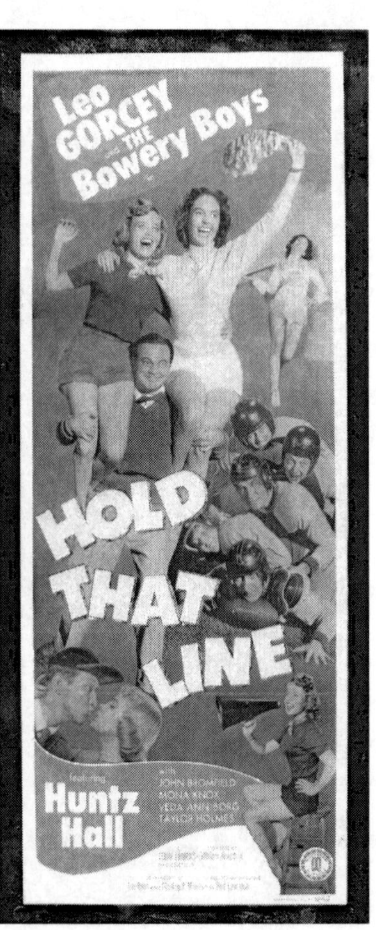

Insert for Hold That Line

Hold that Line lobby card

Here Come the Marines

Monogram: Released June 29, 1952

<u>Cast</u>: The Bowery Boys, Myrna Dell, James Flavin, Tim Ryan and Paul Maxey.

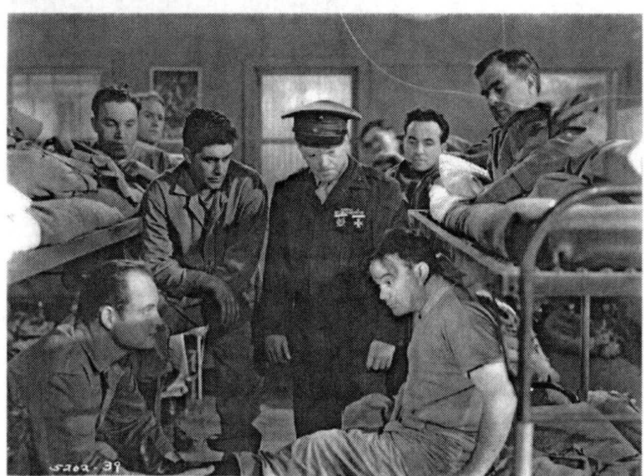

Scene from Here Come the Marines

Poster for Here Come the Marines

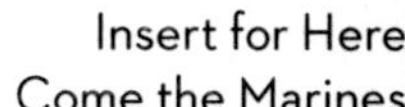

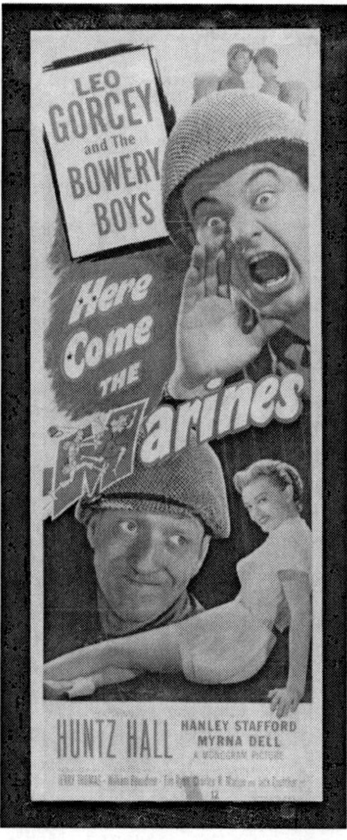

Insert for Here Come the Marines

Feudin' Fools

Monogram: Released September 21, 1952

<u>Cast</u>: The Bowery Boys, Bob Easton, Anne Kimbell, Dorothy Ford, Benny Baker, Oliver Blake, O.Z. Whitehead, Fuzzy Knight and Lyle Talbot.

4 lobby cards from Feudin' Fools

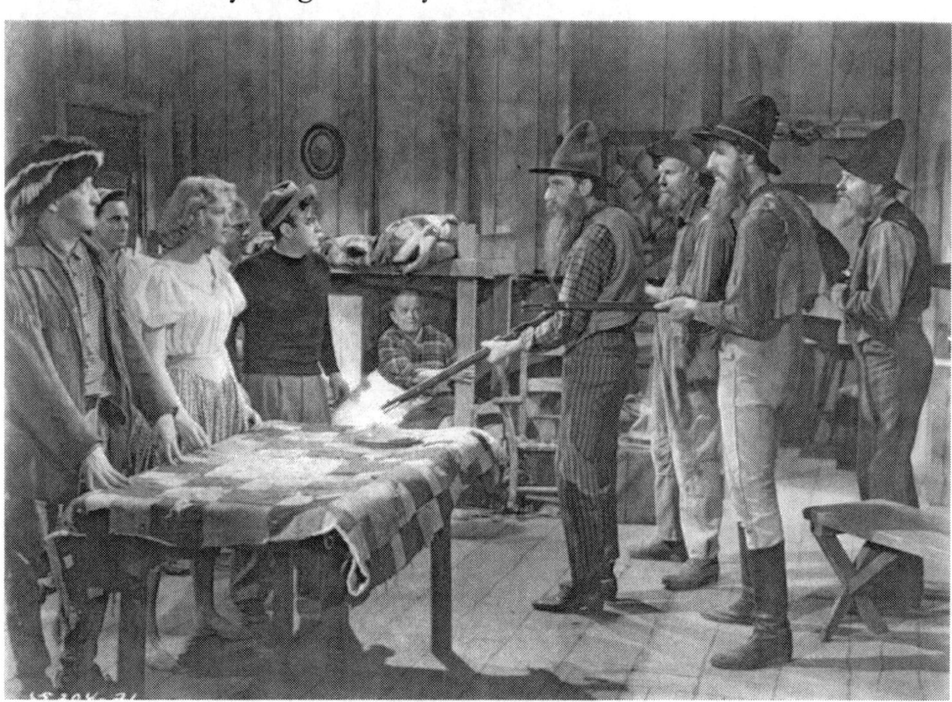

Scene from Feudin' Fools

No Holds Barred

Monogram: Released November 23, 1952

<u>Cast</u>: The Bowery Boys, Marjorie Reynolds, Terrible Tova, Barbara Gray and Henry Kulky.

No Holds Barred Poster

Scene from No Holds Barred

Lobby card from No Holds Barred

Scene still from No Holds Barred

Scene for the film No Holds Barred

Jalopy

Allied Artists: Released February 15, 1952

<u>Cast</u>: The Bowery Boys, Jane Easton, Richard Benedict, Murray Alper, Leon Belasco, Mona Knox and Conrad Brooks.

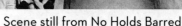

Lobby card for Jalopy

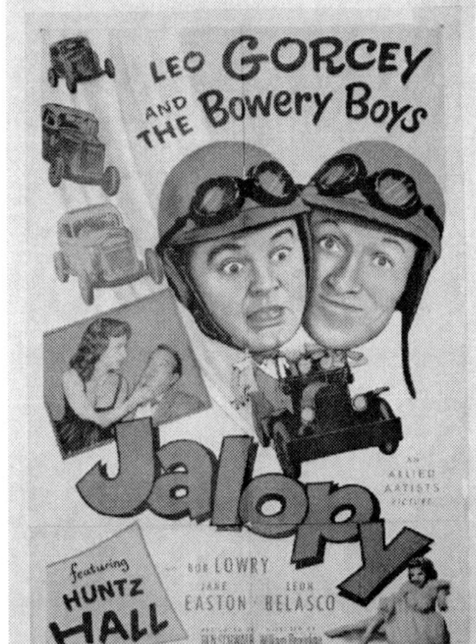

One sheet poster for Jalopy

Scene for the film Jalopy

Scene from Jalopy

Insert for Jalopy

Loose in London

Allied Artists: Released May 24, 1953

Cast: The Bowery Boys, Walter Kingsford, Angela Greene, John Dodsworth, Joan Shawlee and Rex Evens.

Poster for Loose in London

Lobby card from Loose in London

Scene from Loose in London

Clipped Wings

Allied Artists: Released August 14, 1953

Cast: The Bowery Boys, Renie Riano, June Vincent, Todd Karns, Mary Treen, Frank Richards, Jeanne Dean and Elaine Riley.

Poster for Clipped Wings

Lobby card for Clipped Wings

Clipped Wings press book

Insert for Clipped Wings

Scene from Clipped Wings

Private Eyes

Allied Artists: Released December 6, 1953

Cast: The Bowery Boys, Rudy Lee, Joyce Holden, Robert Osterloh, William Forrest, Gil Perkins, Chick Chandler and Lee Van Cleef.

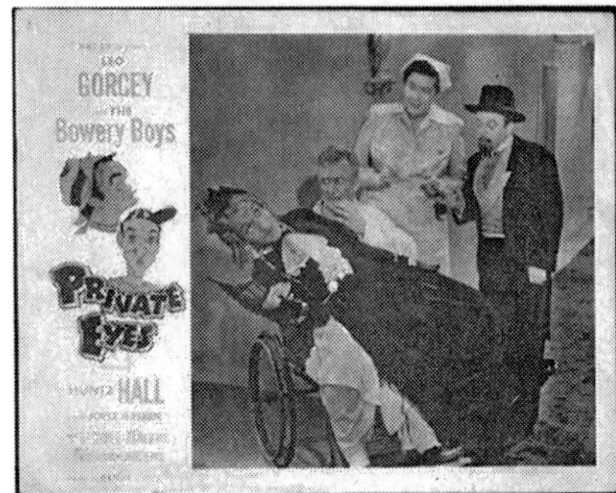

LEO GORCEY
THE
Bowery Boys
PRIVATE EYES
HUNTZ HALL

Lobby card for Private Eyes

Private Eyes one sheet poster

Private Eyes insert

Paris Playboys

Allied Artists: Released March 5, 1954

Cast: The Bowery Boys, Veola Vonn, Steven Geray, Marianne Lynn and John Wengraf.

Scene from Paris Playboys

Paris Playboys one sheet poster

Scene for the film Paris Playboys

Scene still from Paris Playboys

The Bowery Boys Meet the Monsters

Allied Artists: Released June 6, 1954

Cast: The Bowery Boys, John Dehner, Lloyd Corrigan, Ellen Corby, Paul Wexler and Laura Mason.

Scene from The Bowery Boys Meet the Monsters

8 lobby cards for the film The Bowery Boys Meet the Monsters

6 sheet poster from The Bowery Boys Meet the Monsters

Jungle Gents

Allied Artists: Released September 5, 1954

Cast: The Bowery Boys, Patrick O'Moore, Laurette Luez, Woody Strode Murry Alper and Clint Walker.

Poster for Jungle Gents

Jungle Gents still

Press book for Jungle Gents

Huntz Hall, Clint Walker and Laurette Luez in this publicity still from Jungle Gents

Leo Gorcey in Jungle Gents

Bowery to Bagdad

Allied Artists: Released January 2, 1955

Cast: The Bowery Boys, Joan Shawlee, Dick Wessel, Rick Vallin and Robert Bice.

Bowery to Bagdad lobby card

One sheet poster

High Society

Allied Artists: Released April 17, 1955

Cast: The Bowery Boys, Amanda Blake, Dayton Lummis, Addison Richards, Kem Dibbs and Paul Harvey.

Lobby card from High Society

High Society poster

Lobby card for High Society

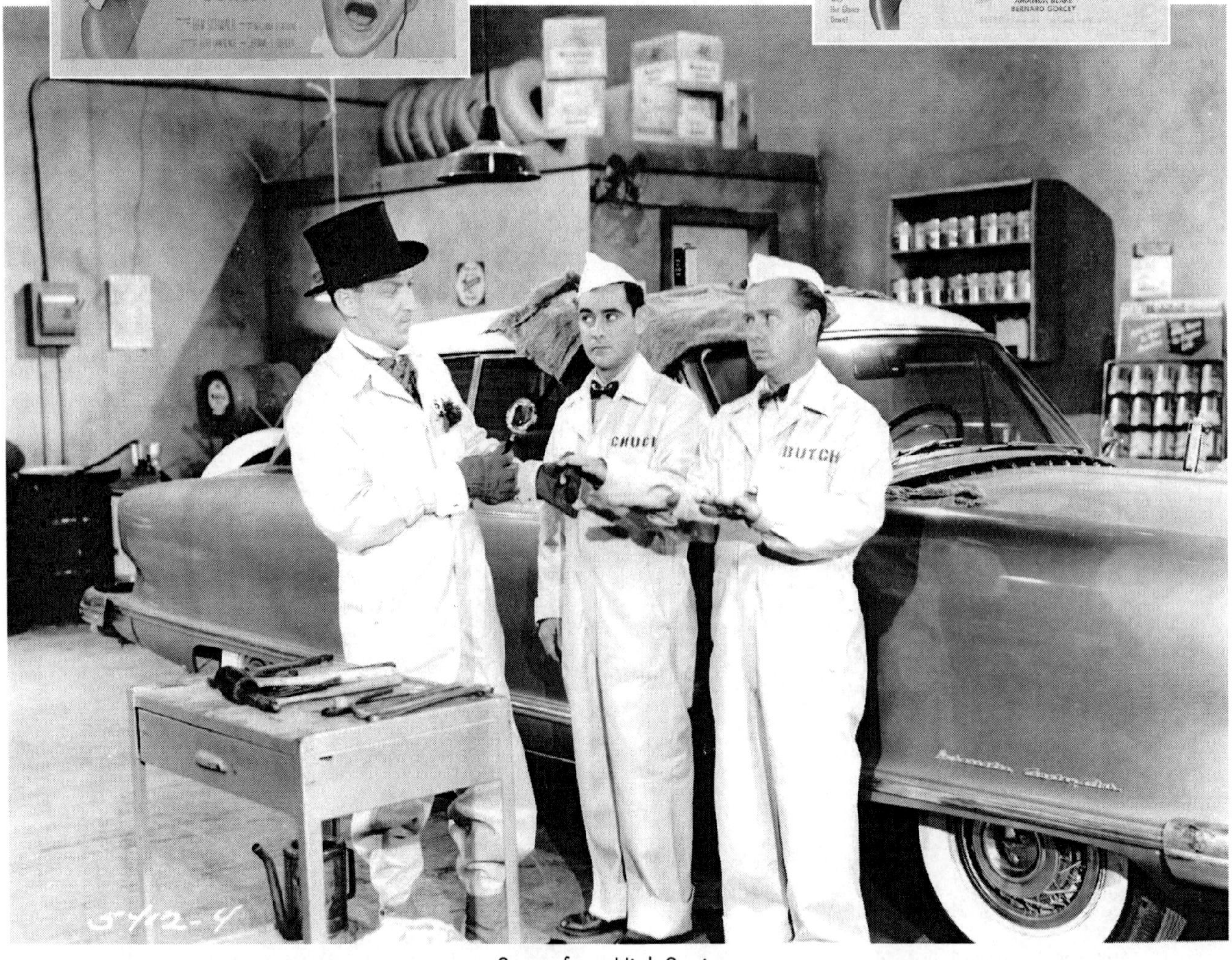

Scene from High Society

Spy Chasers

Allied Artists: Released July 31, 1955

Cast: The Bowery Boys, Leon Askins, Sig Ruman, Veola Vonn, Linda Bennett and Richard Benedict.

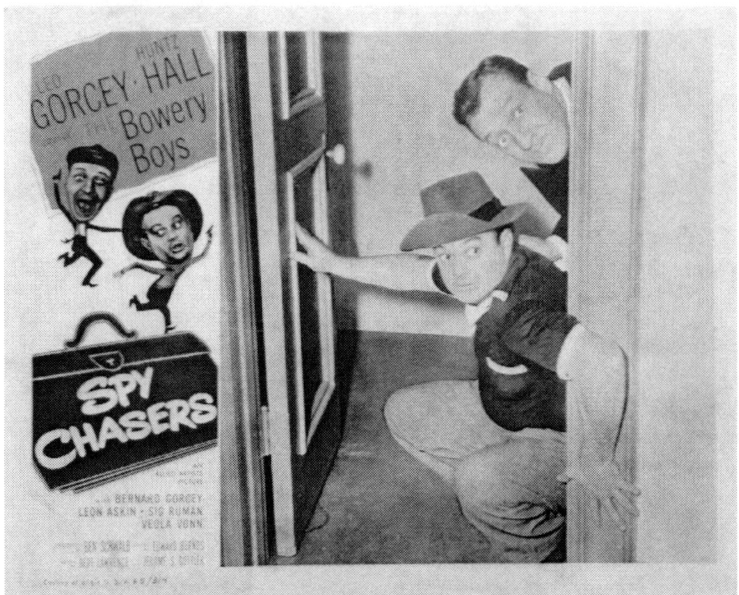

Lobby card for Spy Chasers

Scene from the film Spy Chasers

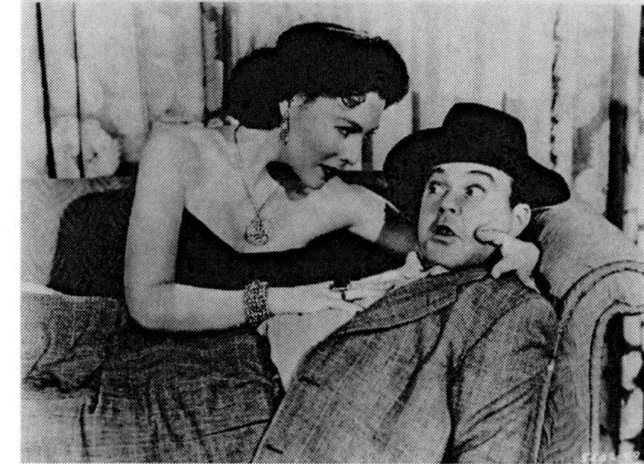

Scene from Spy Chasers.

Jail Busters

Allied Artists: Released September 18, 1955

Cast: The Bowery Boys, Lyle Talbot, Barton MacLane, Fritz Feld, Percy Helton and Anthony Caruso.

Scene from Jail Busters

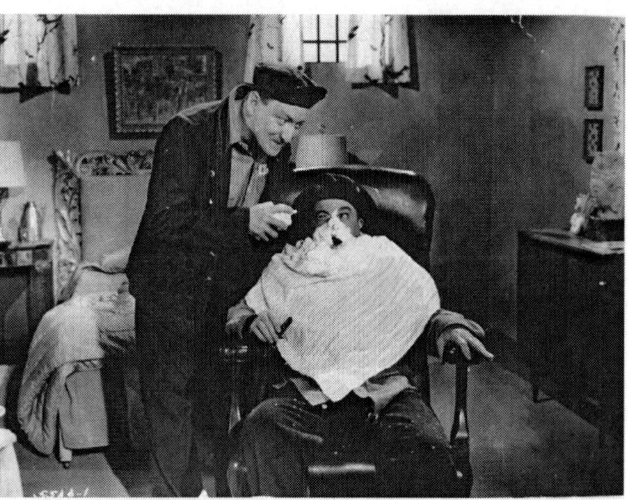

Can you say, i'm no stoolie

Jail Busters one sheet

Scene for the film Jail Busters

Dig That Uranium

Allied Artists: Released January 8, 1956

Cast: The Bowery Boys, Mary Beth Hughes, Raymond Hatton, Myron Healey, Richard Powers and Carl Switzer.

Insert for Dig That Uranium

Dig That Uranium lobby card

Poster for Dig That Uranium

Crashing Las Vegas

Allied Artists: Released April 22, 1956

Cast: The Bowery Boys, Mary Castle, Nicky Blair, Mort Mills and Dick Foote.

Leo Gorcey,Mary Castle and Huntz Hall in this scene from Crashing Las Vegas

Lobby card for Crashing Las Vegas

Scene from Crashing Las Vegas

Crashing Las Vegas poster

Fighting Trouble

Allied Artists: Released September 16, 1956

Cast: The Bowery Boys, Adele Jergens, Joseph Downing, Queenie Smith, Laurie Mitchell, Rick Vallin, Tim Ryan and Danny Welton.

Lobby card from Fighting Trouble

One sheet poster for Fighting Trouble

Hot Shots

Allied Artists: Released December 3, 1956

Cast: The Bowery Boys, Queenie Smith, Philip Phillips, Dennis Moore and Robert Shayne.

Scene from Hot Shots

Half sheet poster for the film Hot Shots

Hot Shots lobby card

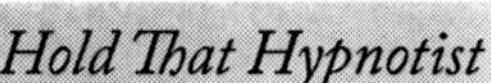

Hold That Hypnotist

Allied Artists: Released February 24, 1957

Cast: The Bowery Boys, Jane Nigh, Queenie Smith, Robert Foulk, Murry Alper and Mel Welles.

Lobby of theater showing Hold That Hypnotist

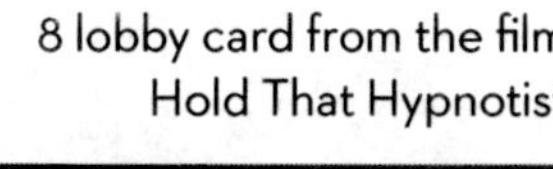

8 lobby card from the film Hold That Hypnotist

Spook Chasers

Allied Artists: Released June 2, 1957

Cast: The Bowery Boys, Percy Helton, Darlene Fields, Bill Henry, Ben Welden and Pierre Watkin.

Lobby card for Spook Chasers

Spook Chasers press book

Spook Chasers lobby card

Stanley Clements and Huntz Hall are all spooked up in this scene

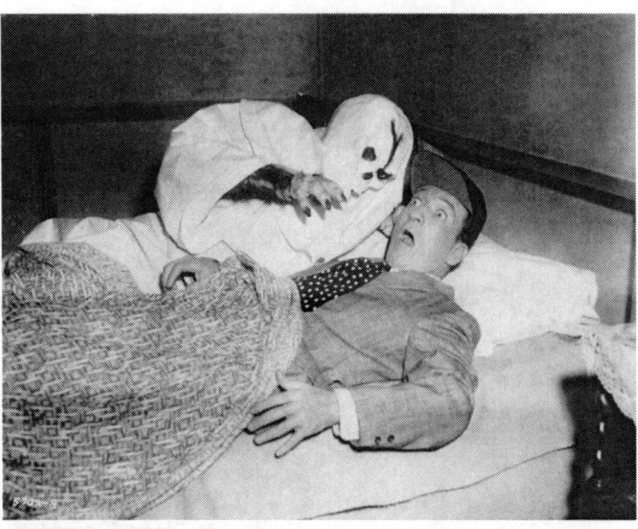

Huntz Hall is all eye's in this scene from Spook Chasers

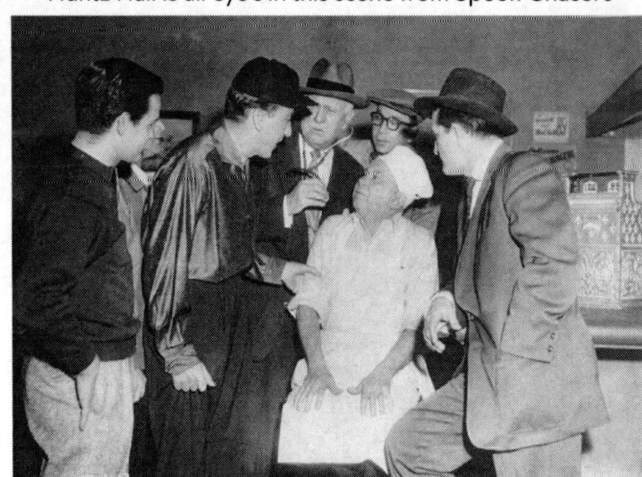

Scene from Spook Chasers

Looking for Danger

Allied Artists: Released October 6, 1957

Cast: The Bowery Boys, Richard Avonde, Otto Reichow, Joan Bradshaw, Lile Kardell and Peter Mamakos.

Looking for Danger lobby card

Huntz Hall looking board in this publicity still from Looking for Danger

Lobby card for Looking for Danger

Looking for Danger scene

Up in Smoke

Allied Artists: Released December 18, 1957

Cast: The Bowery Boys, Judy Bamber, Ric Roman, Byron Foulger, Joe Devlin, James Flavin and Dick Elliott.

Scene from Up In Smoke

Still from Up In Smoke

Rare lobby card for Up In Smoke

Scene for the film Up In Smoke

In the Money

Allied Artists: Released February 16, 1958

<u>Cast</u>: The Bowery Boys, Patricia Donahue, Leonard Penn, John Dodsworth and Dick Elliott.

Scene for In the Money

In the Money lobby card

In the Money lobby card

Scene from In The Money

Scene still for In the Money

CHAPTER 7
The Harlem Dead End Kids Films

I would be remiss if I didn't include The Harlem Dead End Kids, because they were the biggest form of flattery to The Dead End Kids.

The Harlem Dead End Kids made only a couple of films, with titles like *Take My Life* (also known as *Murder Rap*), *Prison Camp* and *Wanted for Murder.*

Lobby card from the film Prison Bait

These films featured an all-black cast. When the films were released to movie theaters, the posters and lobby cards read "an all Colored cast."

The Harlem Dead End Kids were also known as the Harlem Tuff Kids.

These were The Harlem Dead End Kids:

DeForest Covan
Monte Hawley
Freddie Jackson
Eugene Jackson
Paul White
Eddie Lynn

The Harlem Dead End Kids (aka tuff kids) ,lobby card

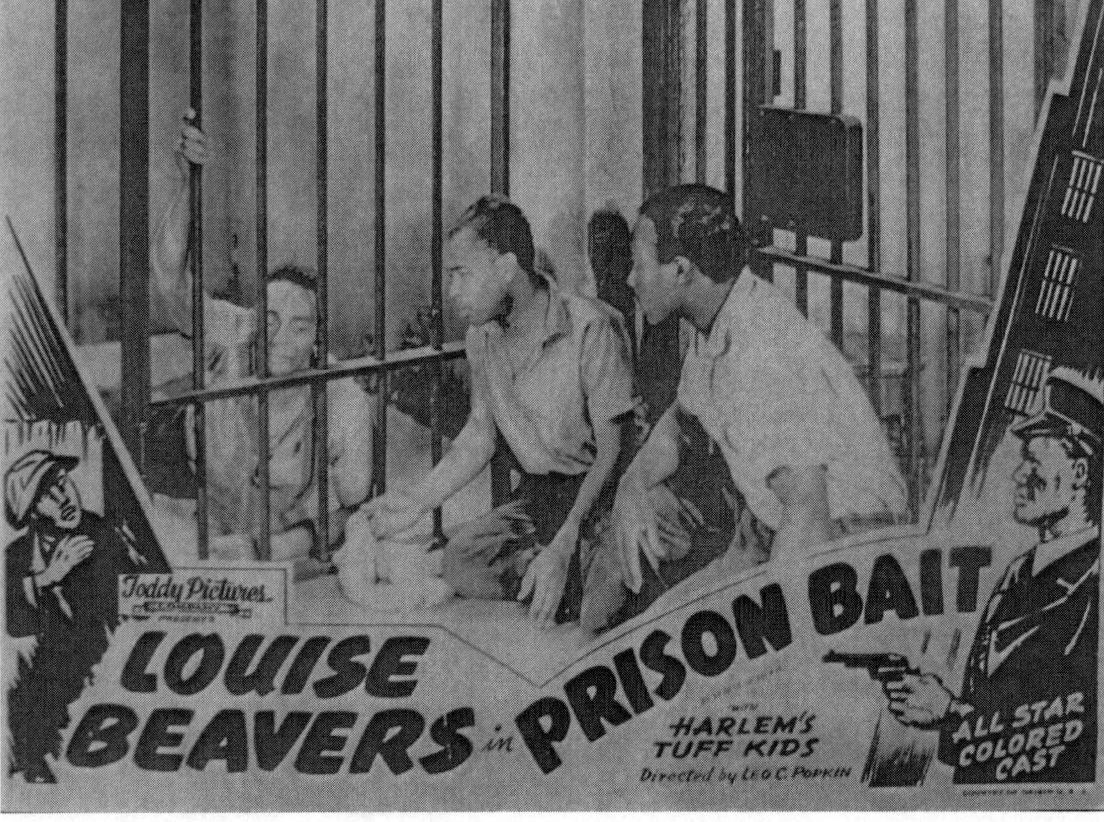

Lobby card for Prison Bait

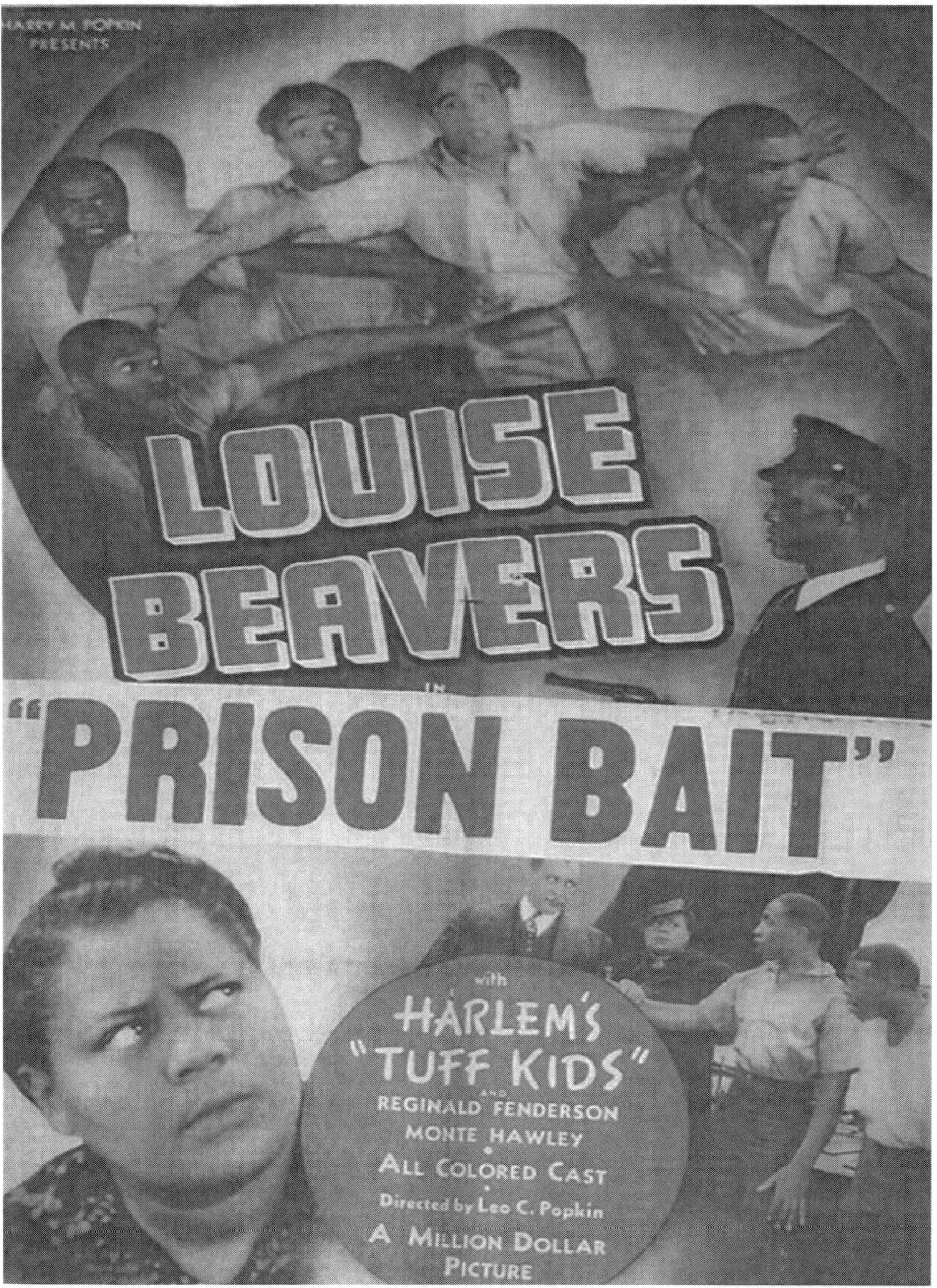

Poster for the film Prison Bait,staring The Harlem Dead End Kids, originally released title Reform School

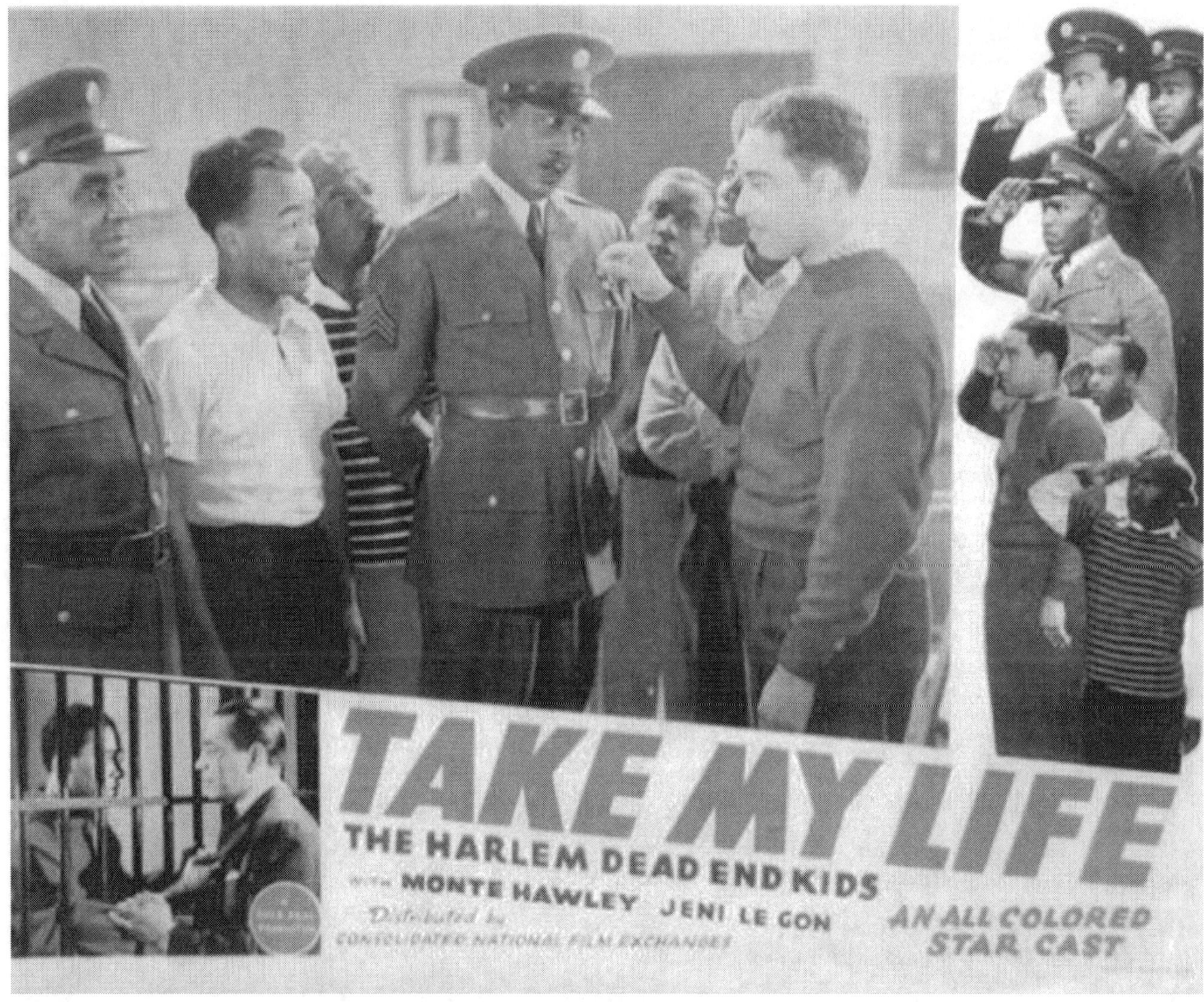

The Harlem Dead End Kids in the film Take My Life

CHAPTER 8
Magazines that ran articles on the Dead End Kids/Little Tough Guys/East Side Kids and Bowery Boys

The World of Yesterday,1978

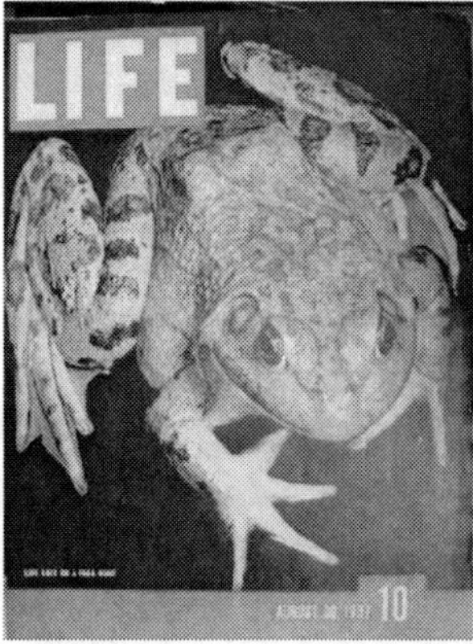

1937 issue of Life Magazine, first magazine to run an article on the Dead End Kids

Best of Filmfax

Boy's Cinema, Crime School, 1938

1938 Radio Stars

Boy's Cinema,May 1939

Boys Cinema-Juvenile Court, 1939

1939 issue of Screen Romances

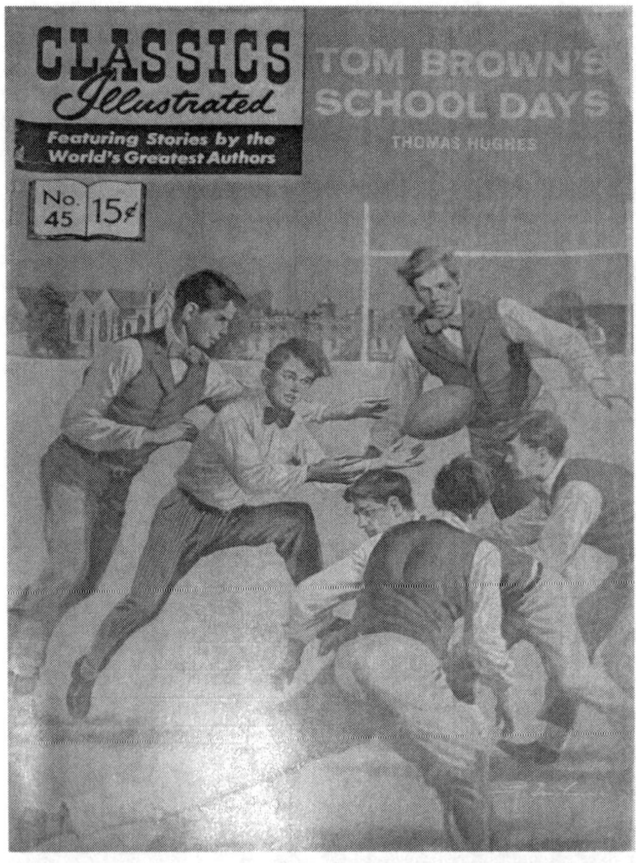

Classics Illustrated,Tom Browns School Days

Colliers,1939

Comic photo from news paper,1938

Film Weekly,1939

Fashin,1939

Fantastic Monsters, 1962

FilmFax,2006

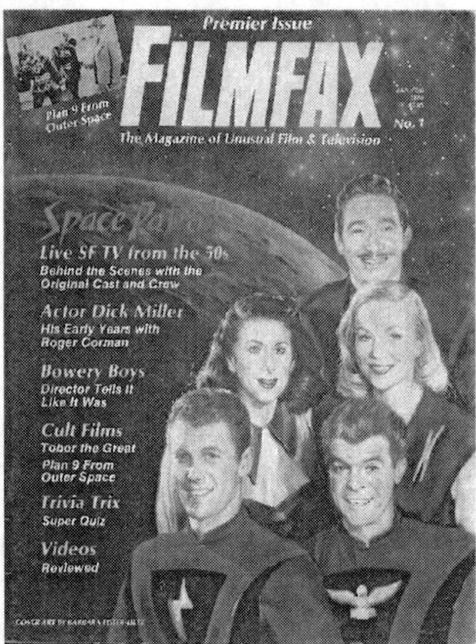

FilmFax # 1

Hollywood, 1938

Hollywood, 1939

Look Magazine, 1939

Films of the Golden age,2007

Films of the Golden Age,Summer 2013,issue 73

Hollywood Pic, 1939

Hollywood Studio Magazine, 1978

Funny Business- winter issue, 1982

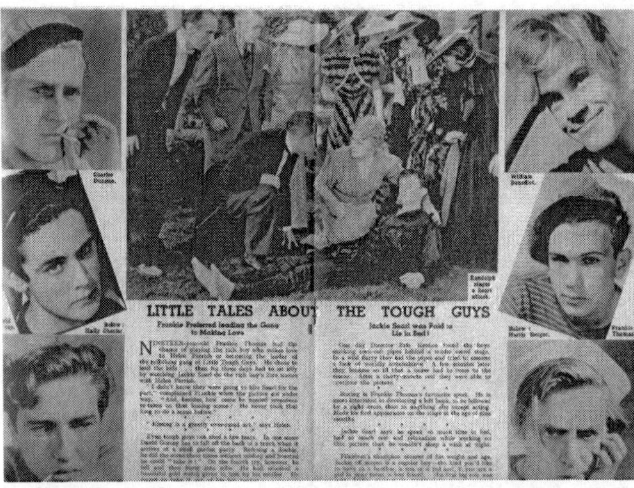
LITTLE TALES ABOUT THE TOUGH GUYS

Magazine inside cover showing the Little Tough Guys in Society, 1938

Modern Movies, 1937

Movie Mirror, 1938

Movie Story, 1939

Pic, 1940

Movie Club

Silver Screen, July 1939

MOVIE MIRROR

Men Adore

SPARKLING HAIR!

Do as hosts of women do . . . complete every shampoo with Nestle Colorinse. Just a quick rinse to give your hair lively gloss . . . and dancing highlights that the camera catches.

Colorinse adds new beauty. Accentuates natural highlights in youthful hair. Gives a richer tone to faded or gray hair.

Among the twelve Colorinse shades there is one to give your hair a flattering tint . . . and glorious sparkle! See Nestle Color Chart at nearest toilet goods counter, *today!* Get 2 rinses for 10c in 10-cent stores; or 5 rinses 25c at drug and department stores.

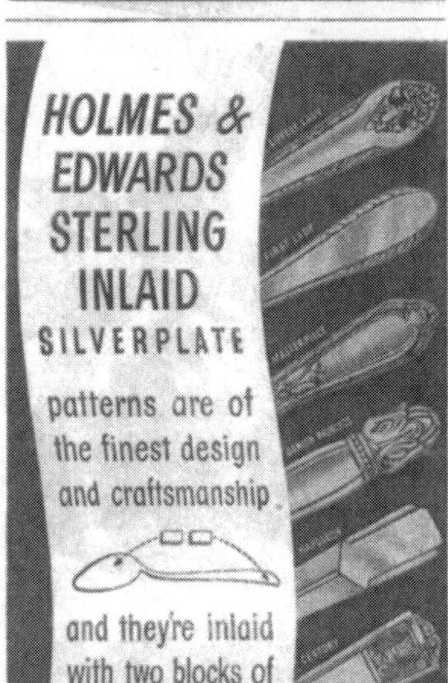

BILLY HALOP,

Guest Editor

HI, JUNIORS:

This is Billy Halop writing you this letter, with the rest of the gang leaning over my shoulder and telling me just what to say about them. So here goes.

Leo Gorcey says I should start off with him because he's the oldest. He's twenty-one, but he doesn't look it. He looks the toughest, I think, and tries to act the hardest-boiled, but the low-down is that he writes poetry! His greatest ambition is to be a writer.

He's worked in a lot of outside pictures, too. He was Joan Crawford's brother in "Mannequin" and he was in "Beloved Brat," "Portia on Trial" and several others.

Leo really is pretty tough because he was fired out of about six grammar schools and three high schools when he was a kid, and the studio had to have a throttle-governor put on his car to keep him down to forty miles an hour. He's a good driver, although he has an awful yen for speed. His father was on the stage and Leo started out by acting in all the plays at Monroe High School in New York. He loves playing "rats" in pictures.

Although Billy Halop writes it, all the "Dead End" boys—left to right, Leo Gorcey, Bernard Punsley, Huntz Hall, Billy himself, Bobby Jordan and Gabriel Dell—had a hand in the actual editing of your department this month!

Bernard Punsley says it's his turn. Okay. He's the fattest one. I guess he's probably the quietest and most serious of us all. He's fifteen, but he's already decided that he wants to be a bacteriologist, and right now he's studying bacteriology with a private tutor. He likes to stay home and study a lot, but we drag him out with us most of the time.

Bernard wasn't planning to be an actor, but when he was in high school a cousin of his heard that Sidney Kingsley was trying to get boys for the stage play, "Dead End," and he landed one of the parts. So now he's out here with us.

Gabriel Dell started out by playing "Hamlet" in high school. The class wrote their own version of the show and it turned out to be a farce. He made such a hit, though, that his family sent him to the Professional Children's School in New York. On account of the experience he got in dramatic school he landed a part in "The Good Earth" and worked in it for several months before he was engaged for "Dead End." He's crazy about acting, but his big ambition is to be a motion picture director.

Huntz Hall wants to be a movie producer. All you have to do is mention producers around him and he goes nuts—waves his arms in the air and shouts at the top of his voice, "Get me a hundred girls! Build me a million sets! Where's all the drums? I need a thousand elephants!" When all that's over, he subsides and says, "It's a cinch! That's all there is to being a producer!" It's his favorite gag.

Movie Mirror,guest editor Billy Halop, 1938

Picture Play,1938

Mongram Studio, what's new, 1952

Pictorial Previews paper ad for the movie Dead End, 1937

Screen Radio, 1938

Screenbook, 1938

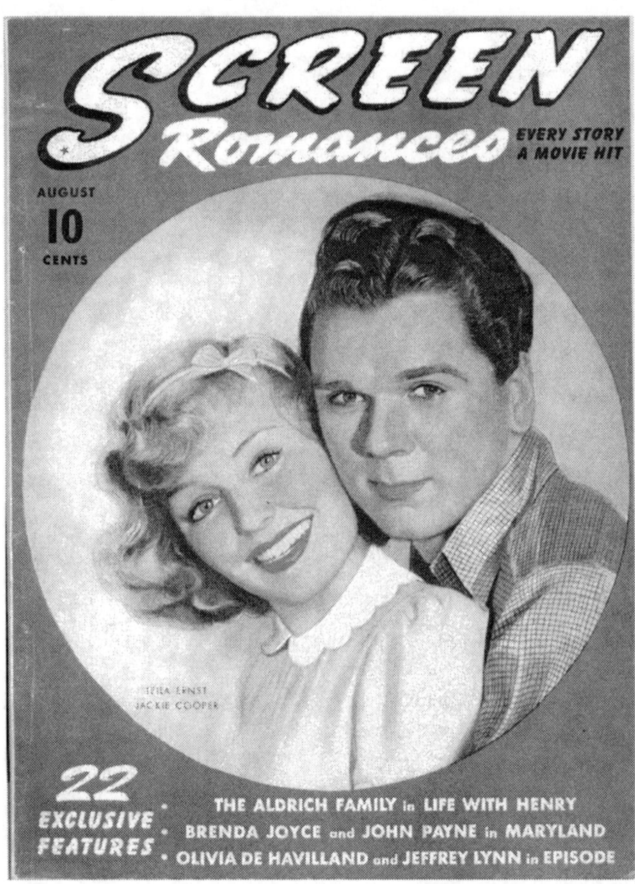

Screen Romances, 1939

TV week,1971

Screen Guide, 1939

Picture Show, 1939

ScreenLand,1938

Screenland, 1970

Screen Pictorial, 1940

The little Tough Guys

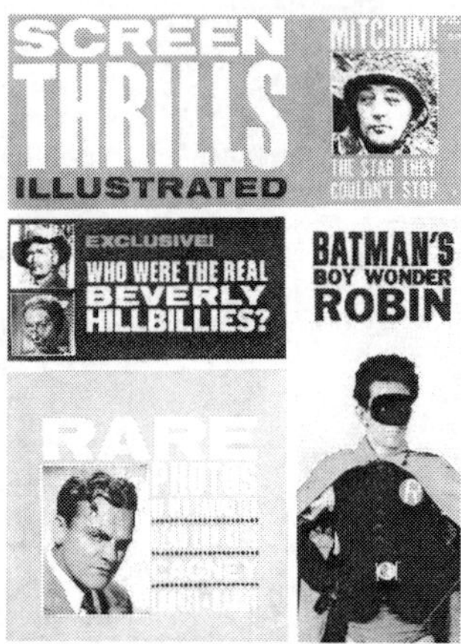

Screen Thrills magazine, July issue

CHAPTER 9
The Many Faces of the Dead End Kids, Little Tough Guys, East Side Kids and The Bowery Boys

Ann Sheridan and Huntz Hall on the set of Angels Wash Their Faces

A very young Jimmy McCallion

6 faces of Gabe Dell

Off the Record lobby card

2 faces of Billy Halop

Frankie Thomas portrait from Flying Cadets

6 faces of Frankie Darro

5 faces of Bernard Punsly

8 faces of Billy Halop

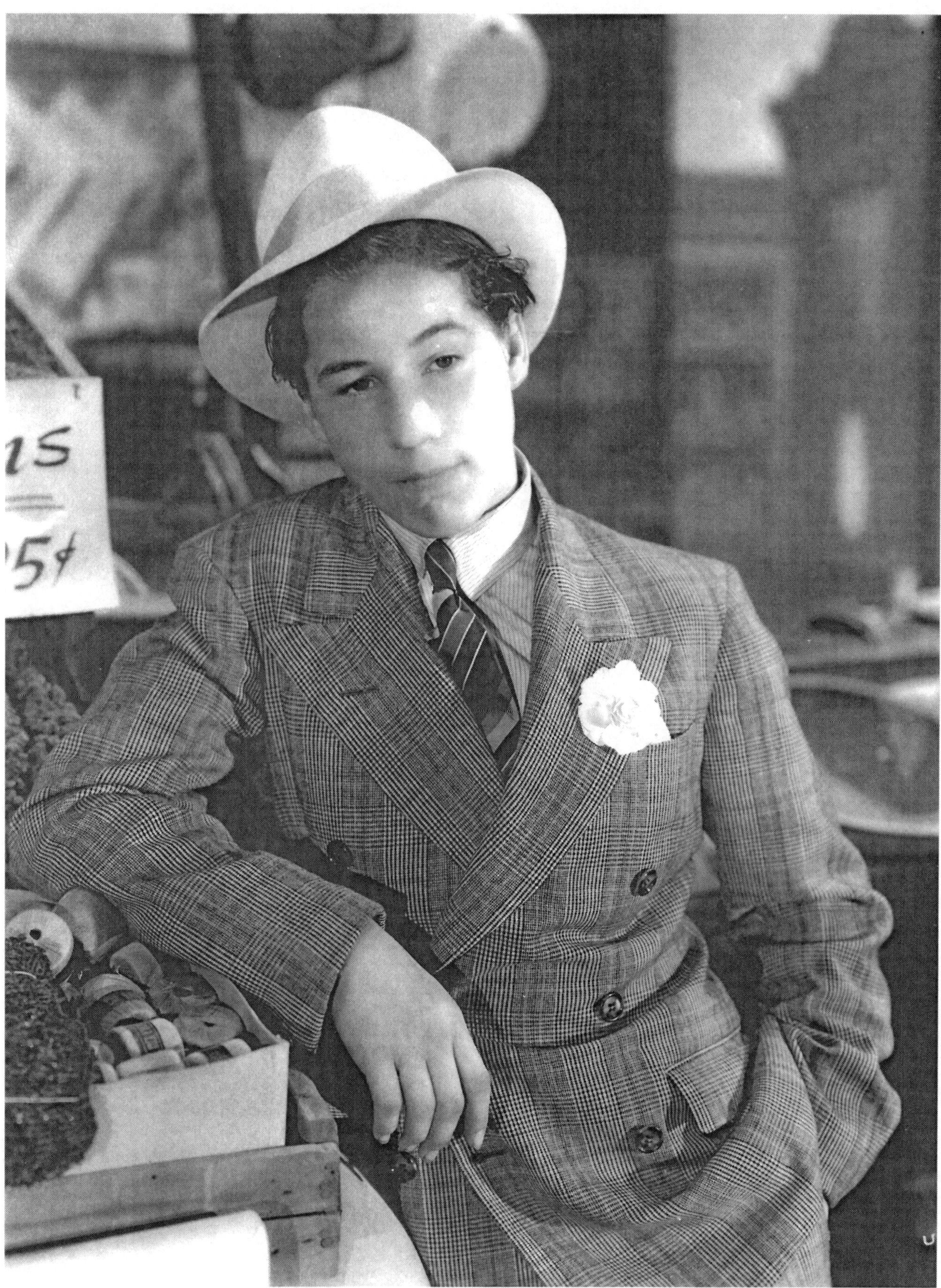

Bobby Jordan in *Off the Record*

Huntz Hall in Little Tough Guy

Leo Gorcey saying so what if I flubeed my lines from the film Dead End

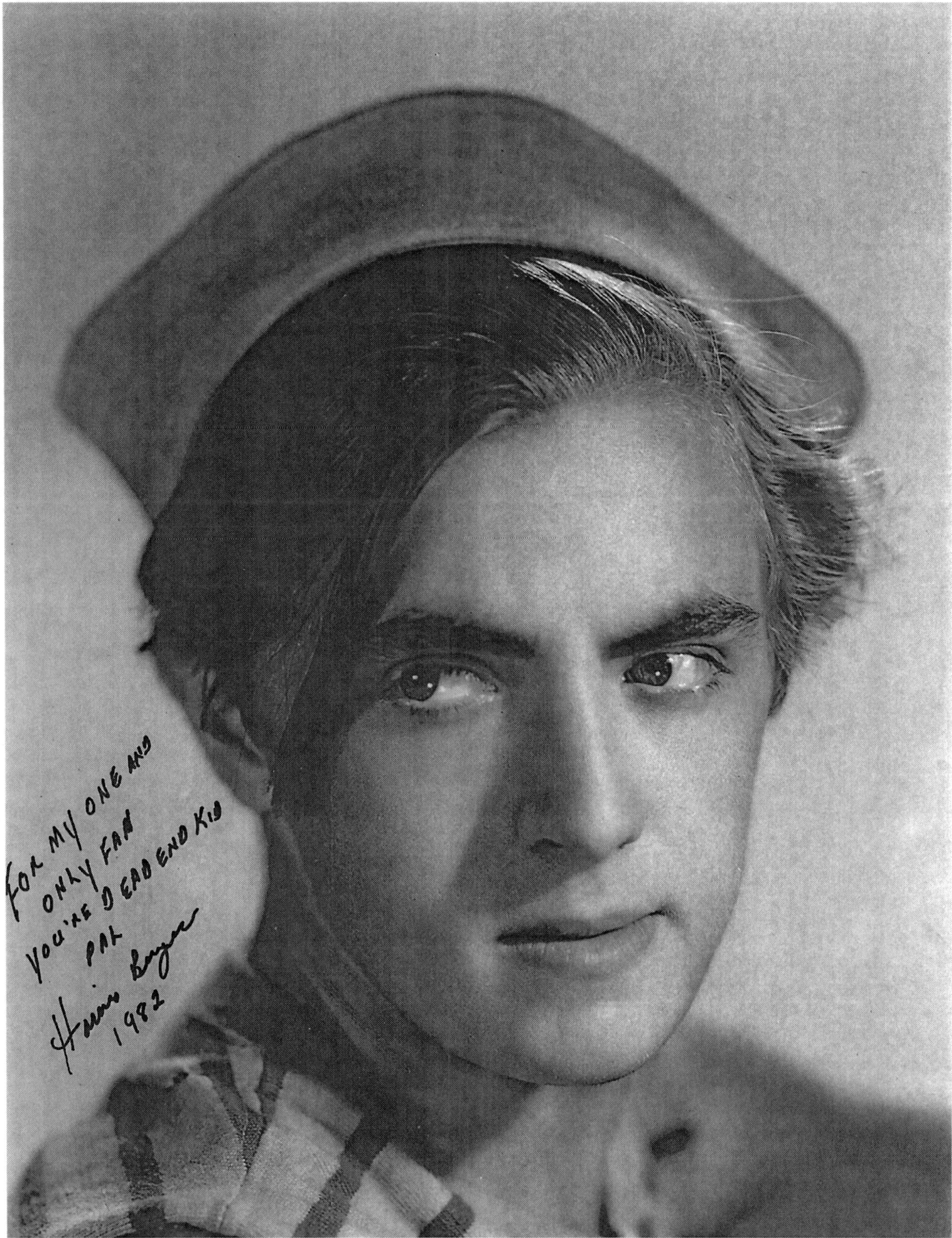
FOR MY ONE AND
ONLY FAN
YOU'RE DEAD END KID
PAL
Harris Berger
1982

Portrait of Harris Berger

Portrait still of Bobby Jordan from the 1940 film Military Academy

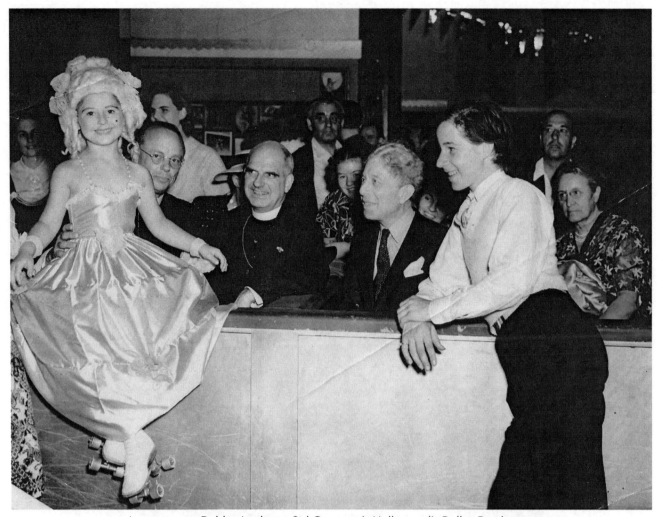

A very young Bobby Jordan at Sid Grauman's Hollywood's Roller Bowl,1930s

Shot Jimmy Strand

A very rare shot of Leo Gorcey with the Hughes Foursome

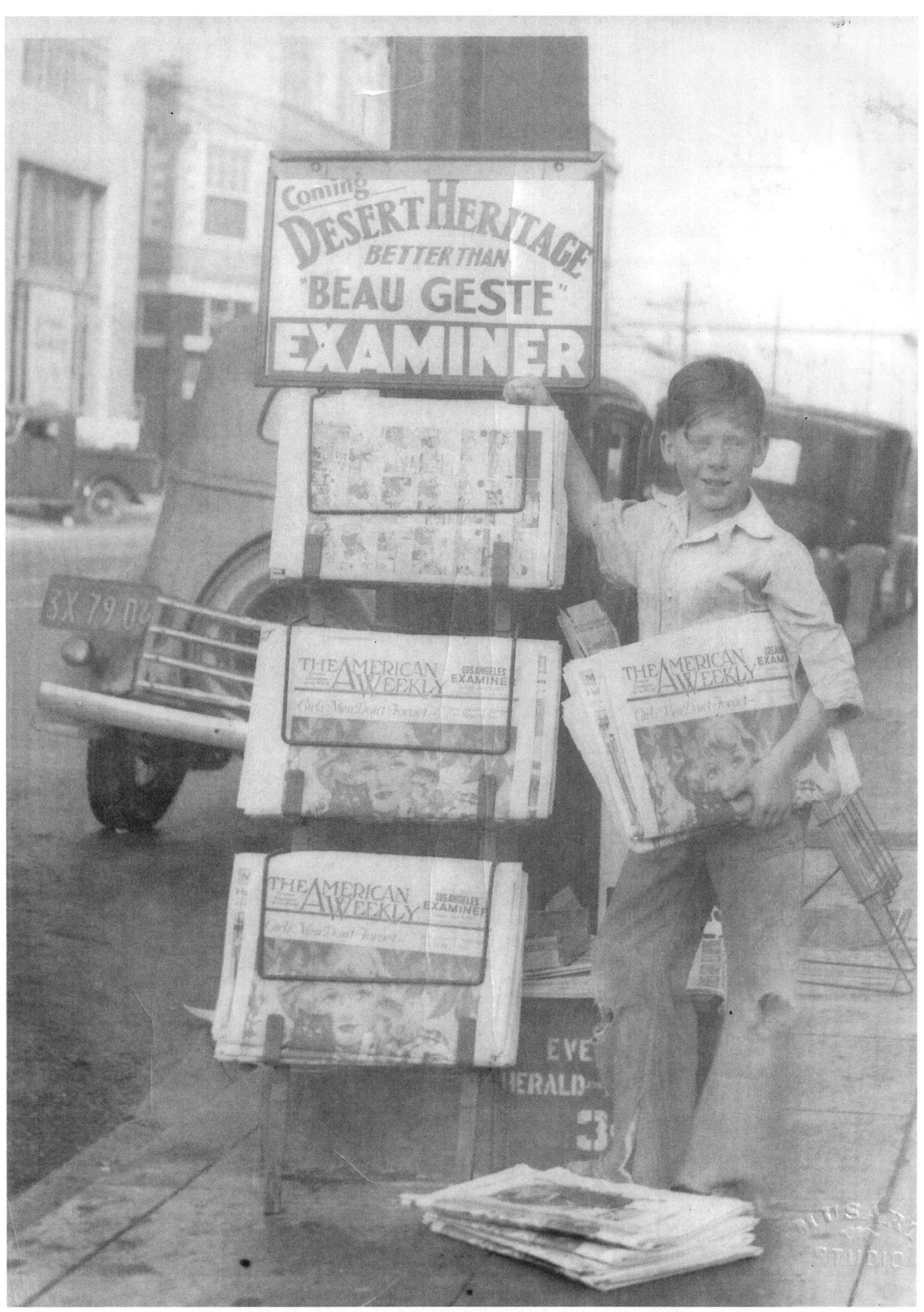

A 7 year old Bennie Bartlett seen here hawking news papers

A very young shot of Billy Halop from his radio days as Bobby Benson

A young Billy Halop as Bobby Benson (radio show)

ARLINGTON TRACK EDITION

ILLINOIS
the Green Sheet
Finest Little Newspaper

50 CENTS 50 CENTS

Sports News

119 SATURDAY, SEPTEMBER 22, 1979

ARLINGTON PARK

First Race 2:00 p.m. – Daily Double 1st and 2nd
Quinellas: 2nd, 4th & 6th Races Trifecta: 9th Race

Starting, Monday, Sept. 24th, Thoroughbred Racing Resumes at Sportsman's Park at 1:30 P.M. Daily Thru End of December

Starting, Monday, Sept. 24th, Harness Racing Moves to Maywood Park at 8 o'clock Nightly Thru End of December

OPEN AND GO TO 2ND RACE, TELL ME IF YOU SEE ANYTHING OF IMPORTANCE. I WOULD LIKE BACK. PHOTOCOPY MACH. IS DOWN

Arlington Horse Track-1979,a horse named Dead End Kid won a race

Bernard Gorcey as he appeared in the film The Set Up with Robert Ryan

Autographed picture of Bernard Punsly and Leo Gorcey

Bennie Bartlett in a scene from the film the Texas Rangers

Bernard Punsly takes dead aim

Hi Richard!
Thanks for being
so nice—
With Love,
Pamela Blake

Beauty Pamela Blake

Billy Halop portrait from the film They Made Me a Criminal

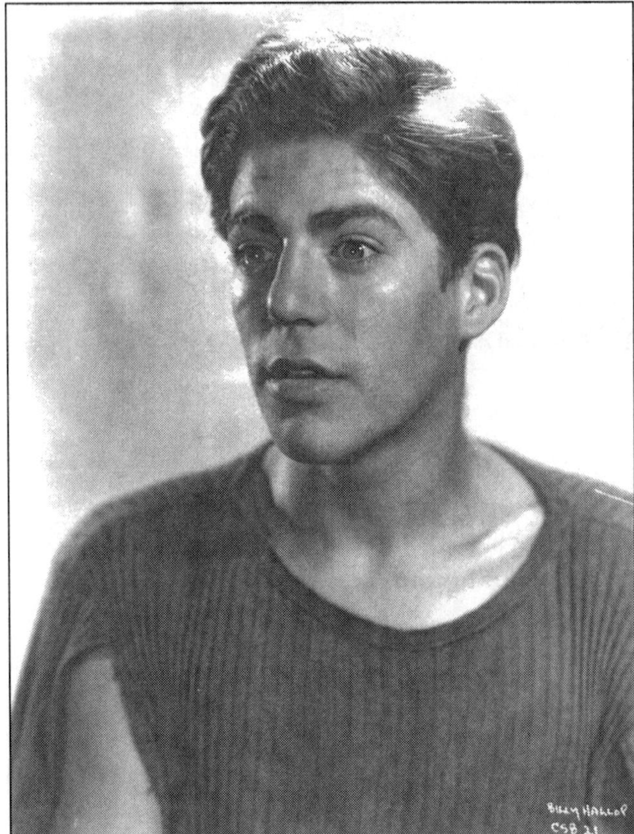

Billy Halop portrait still from Angels With Dirty Faces

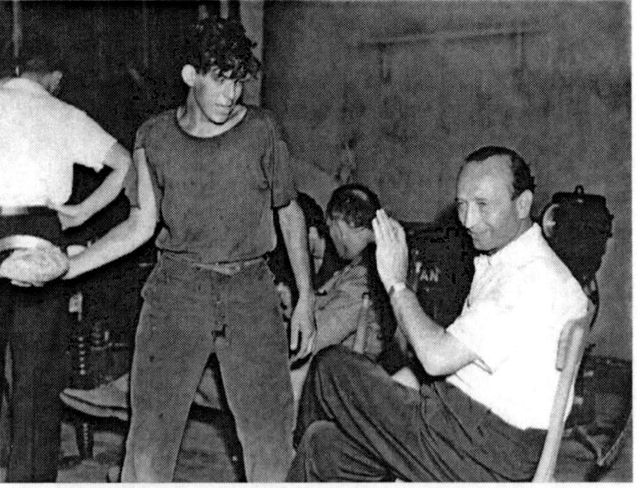

Billy Halop has a pie for director Michael Curtiz

Billy Halop and David Gorcey in this publicity shot from Little Tough Guy

Billy Halop in Junior Army

Billy Benidict in this shot from 1938

Billy Halop in a great shot,showing dispair in this shot

Bernard Punsly, What D'YA Mean, Tough, for his role in Little Tough Guy

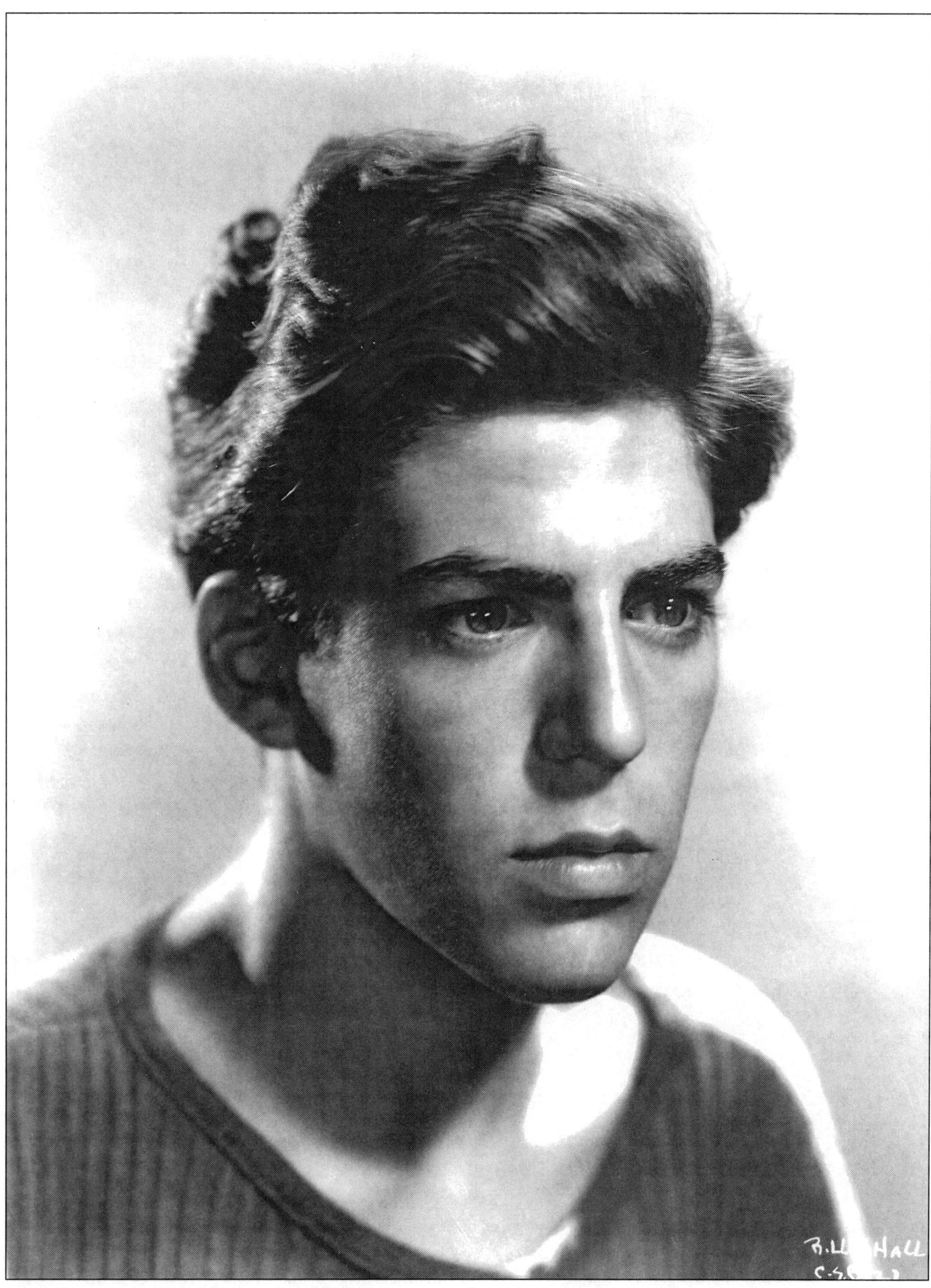

Billy Halop in Angels With Dirty Faces

Billy Halop Looking dapper

Billy Halop-in a nice portrait shot

Billy Halop, in a more serious mood

Bobby Jordan in a scene from the film Off the Record

Bobby Jordan gives Golden Gloves boxer Tony Celentano boxing advice

Bobby Jordan in a publisty shot from Crime School

Bobby Jordan in the film Off the Record

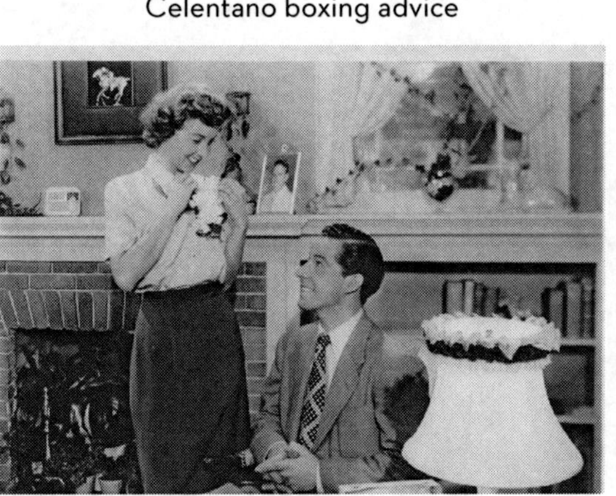

Bobby Jordan in the film short A Watch For Joe

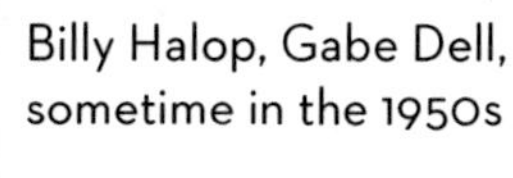

Billy Halop, Gabe Dell, sometime in the 1950s

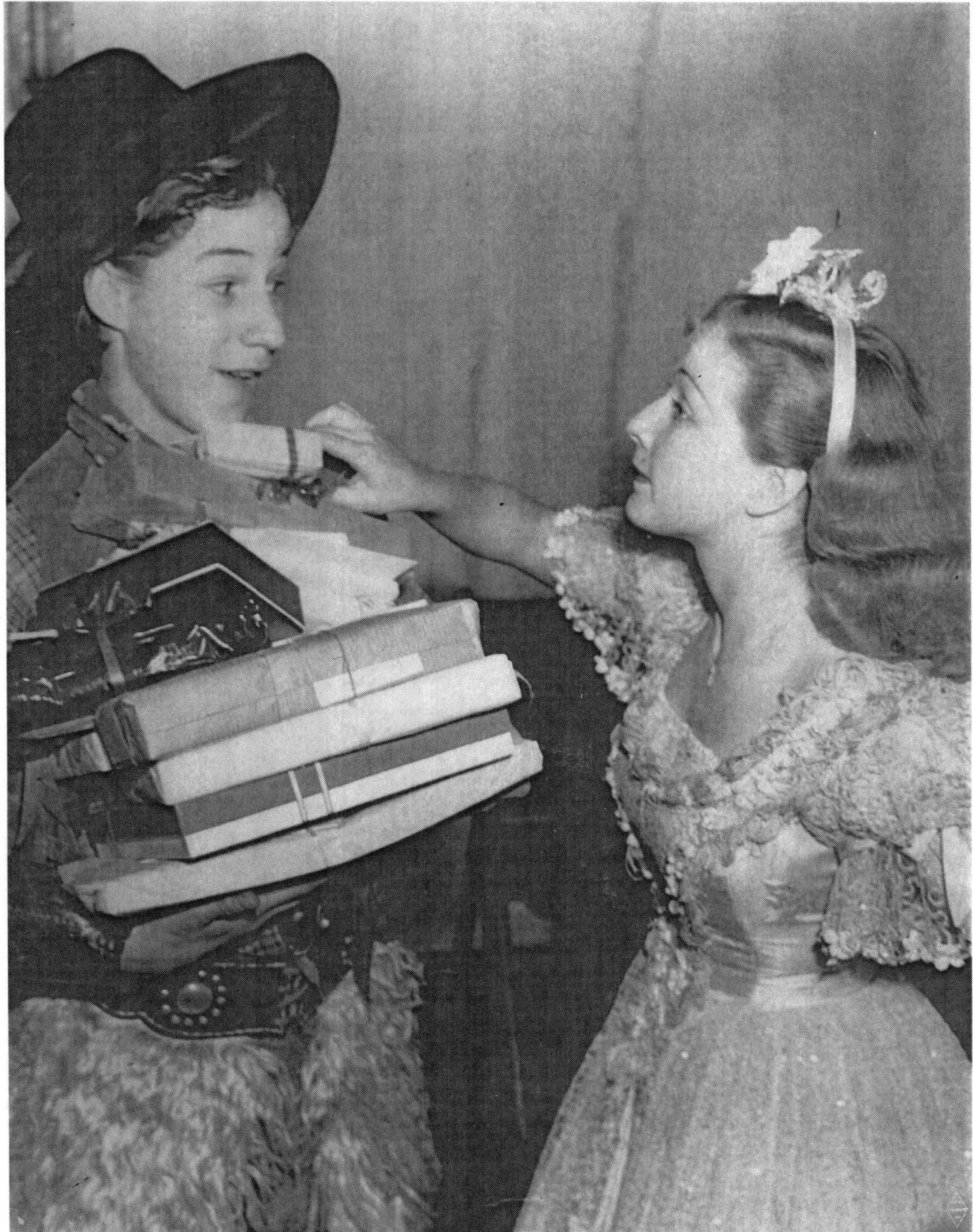

Bobby Jordan pictured here with Boita Granville

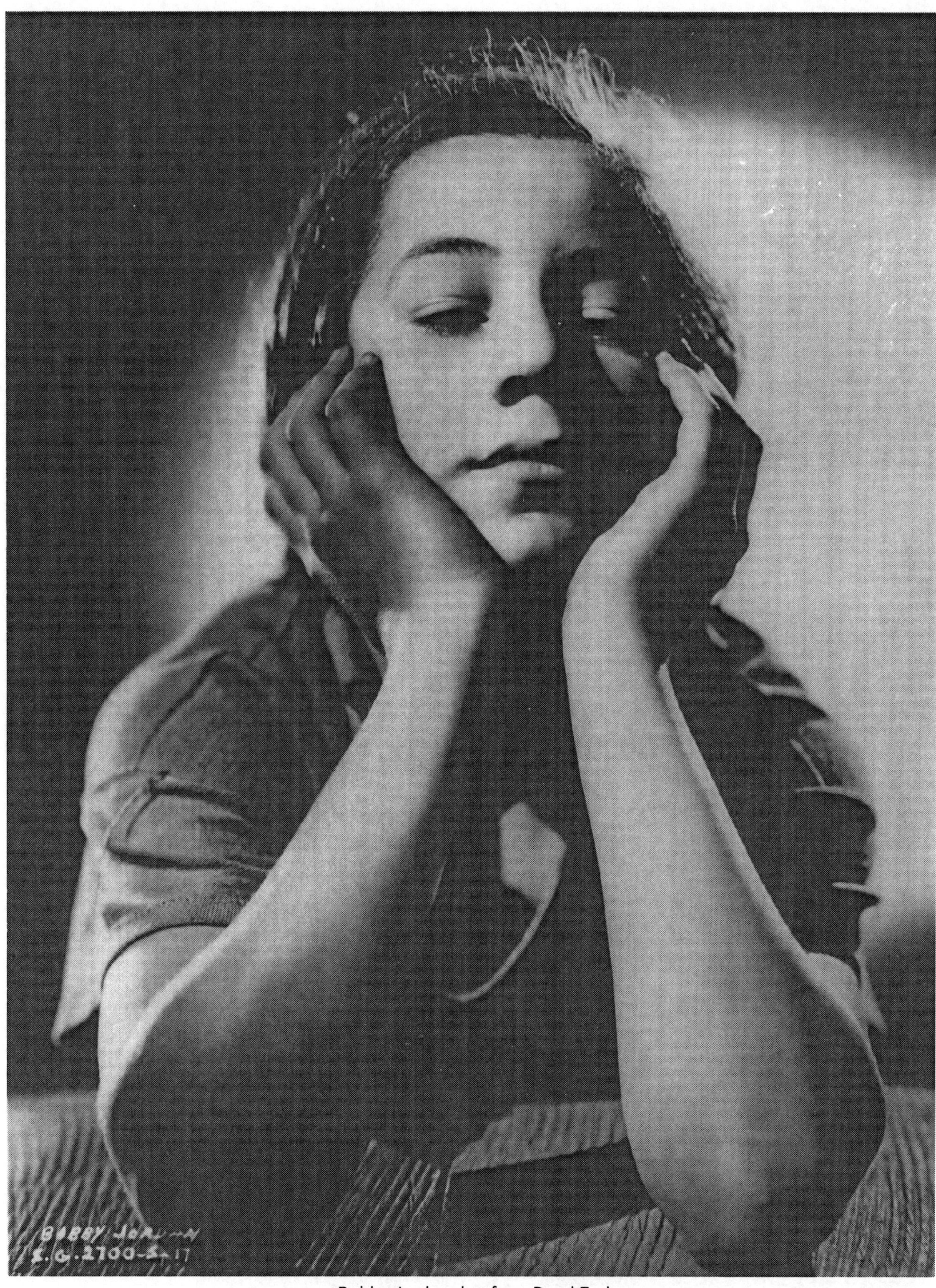

Bobby Jordan shot from Dead End

Bobby Jordan singing at a club, date and where unknown

Buddy Gorman and friend, (2009)

Bobby Stone and Marc Lawrence in a scene from Neath Brooklyn Bridge

Charles Peck

Bobby Stone in Chick Carter, 2nd from right

Bobby Stone and Elvis

Bridgewater film stars of 1939

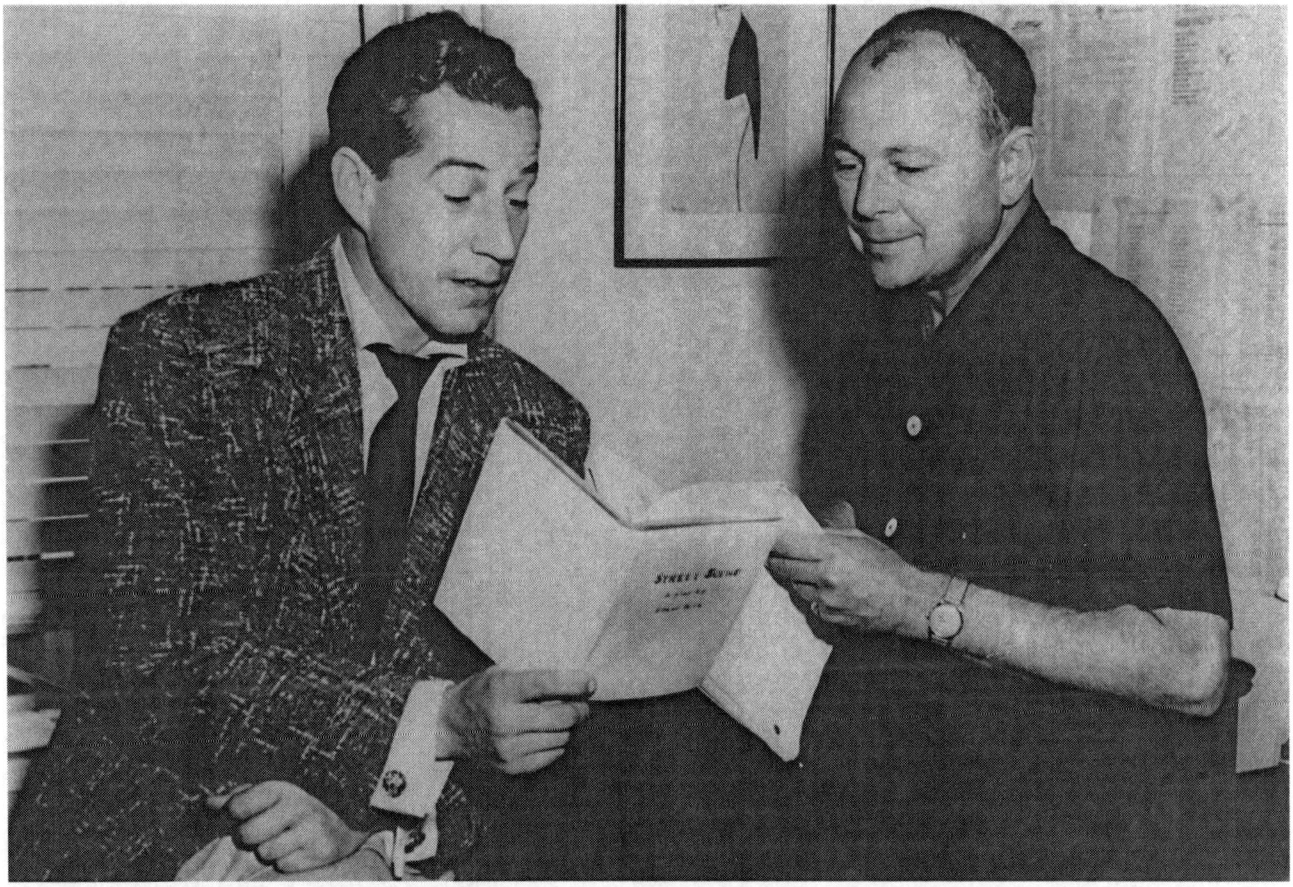

Buster Collier,the voice of Superman on the radio goes over a script with Bobby

Cagney on the set of Angels With Dirty Faces with director Michael Curtiz

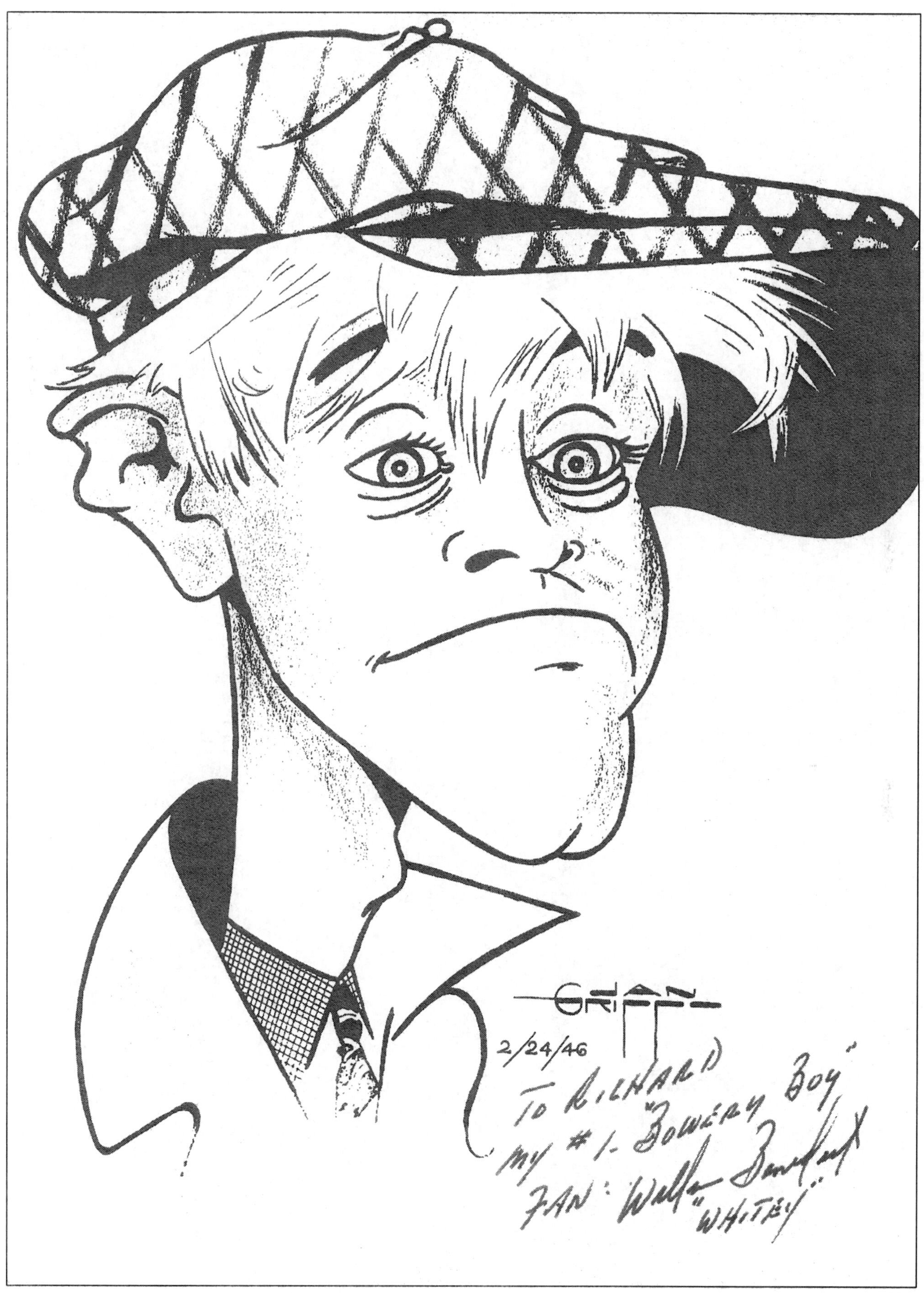

Cartoon picture of Billy Benedict

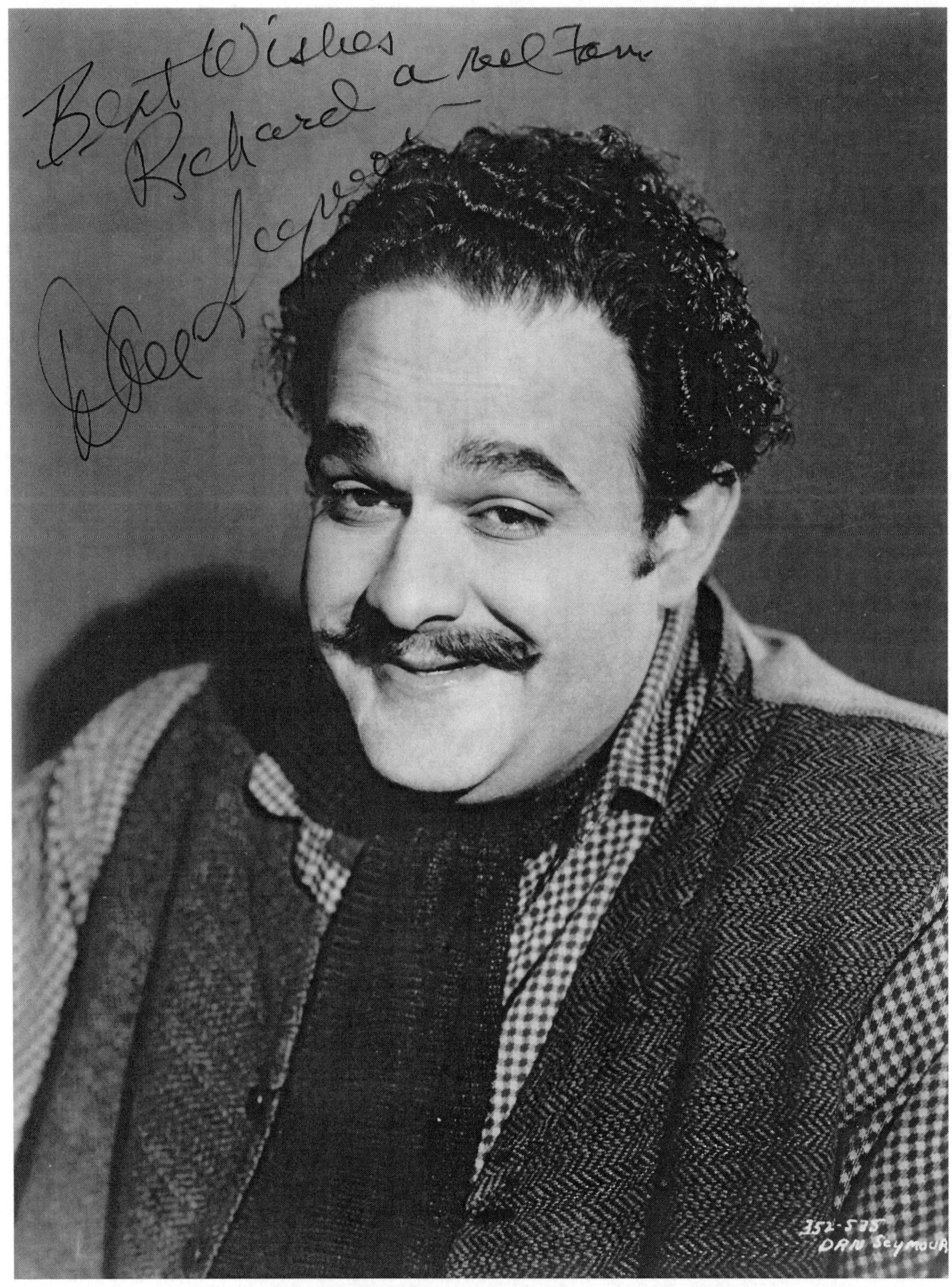

Dan Seymour who played Dr. Armand in the film Hard Boiled Mahoney

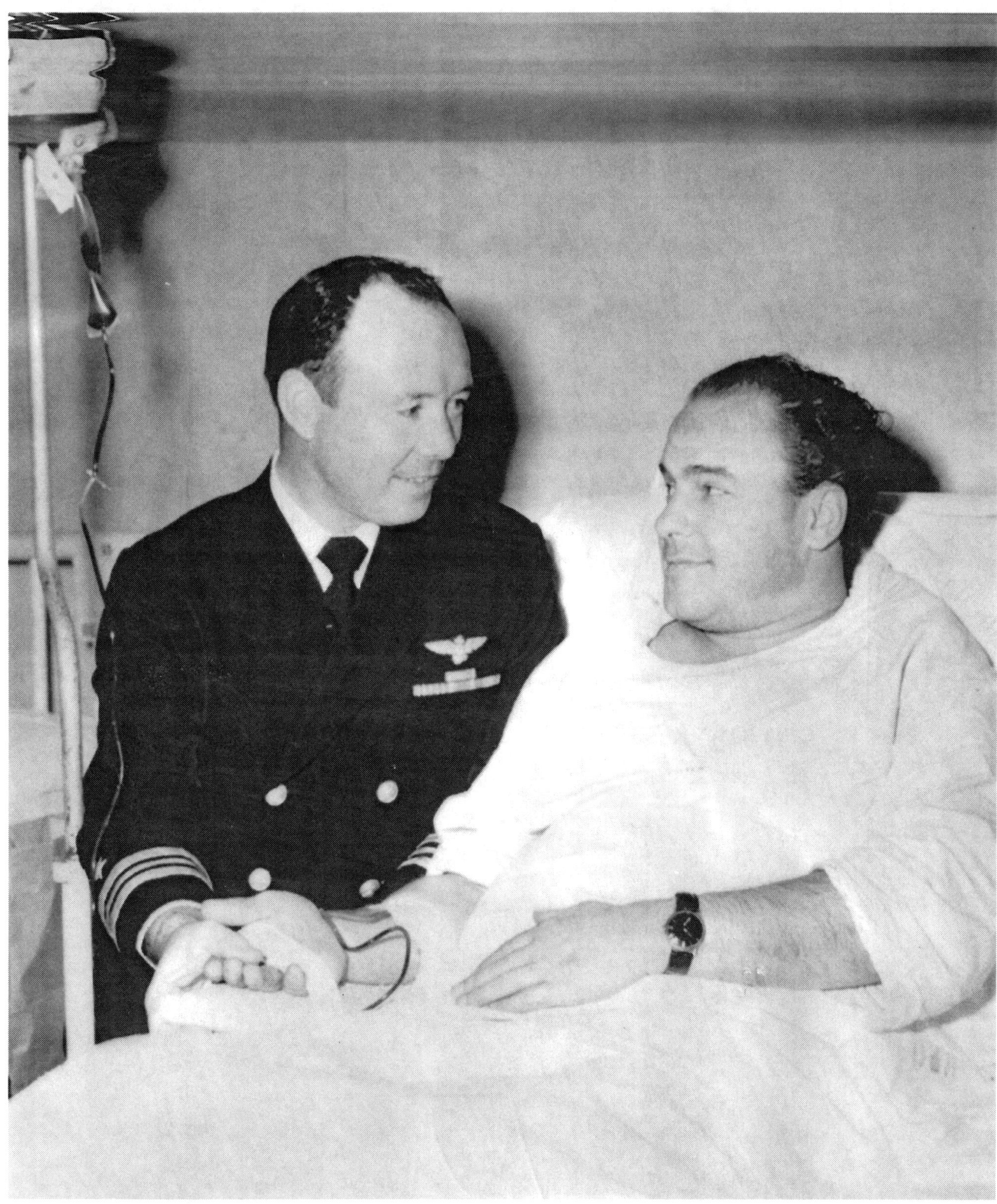

David Durand in need of blood for an operation is greeted by childhood friend Jr. Coghlan

David Durand in the film Song of Love of love

David Gorcey and his Mom Josephine relaxing at David's house

David Gorcey Jr. and son David the 3rd

David Gorcey in his last screen role as a gun fighter in the film Cole Younger Gunfighter

Dell-Bogart and Hall on the set of the film Crime School

David Gorcey as Yap, in Little Tough Guys in Society

David Gorcey strikes a pose for his role in Little Tough Guy

David Gorcey-publicity shot

Dick Chandlee and my wife Mary, He's a real charmer

Dick Chandlee at bottom in the film Tom Brown's School Days

Director Lewis Seiler and Bernard Punsly go over a scene for the film Crime School

Director William Wyler setting up a scene for the film Dead End

Eddie Brian was one of the original East Side Kids

Don't let the funny face's of the kids fool you

Far right is Gabe Dell on the Steve Allen show, circ-1957

F--k You pose

Elisha Cook jr. as Danny in the Little Tough Guy film Newsboys home

Eugene Francis in 1937

Frankie Burke and Wally Wesmore

Frankie Burke looking debonair

Frankie Burke looking much older

From left, Donald Hughes, Miss Mack, Billy Halop, Florence Halop and Lester Yay 2nd from right

Frankie Thomas and actress-dancer Armida do the Tango

Gabe Dell as he appeared in the film Dead End

Gabe Dell and Huntz Hall in Hit the Road

Gabe Dell striks a pose for his role in Crime School

From the film, The Little Tough Guys in Society-If Looks Could Kill!

Gabe Dell in the tv show The Corner Bar

Gabe Dell in the film On Dress Parade

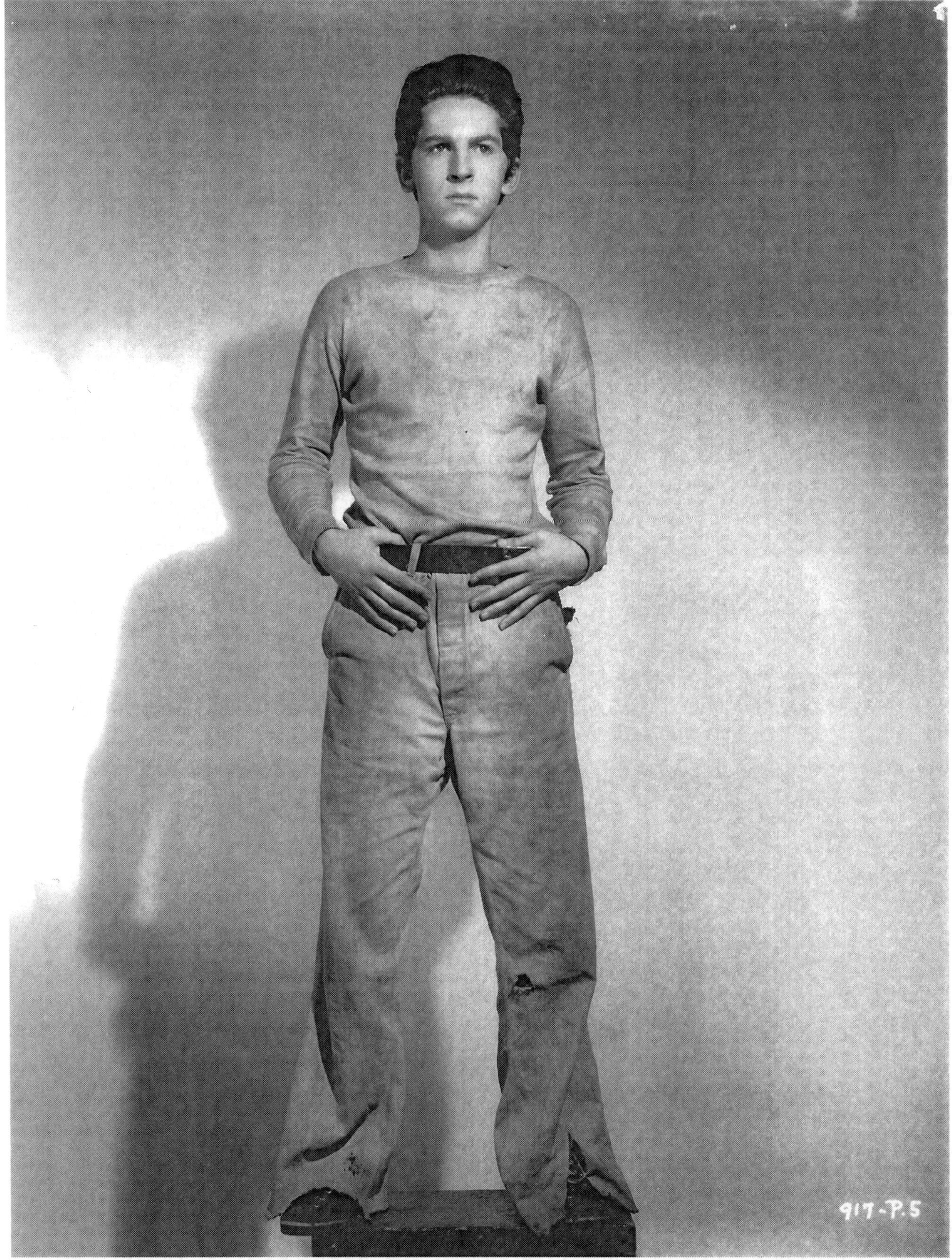

Gabe Dell in Little Tough Guy Tough Guy

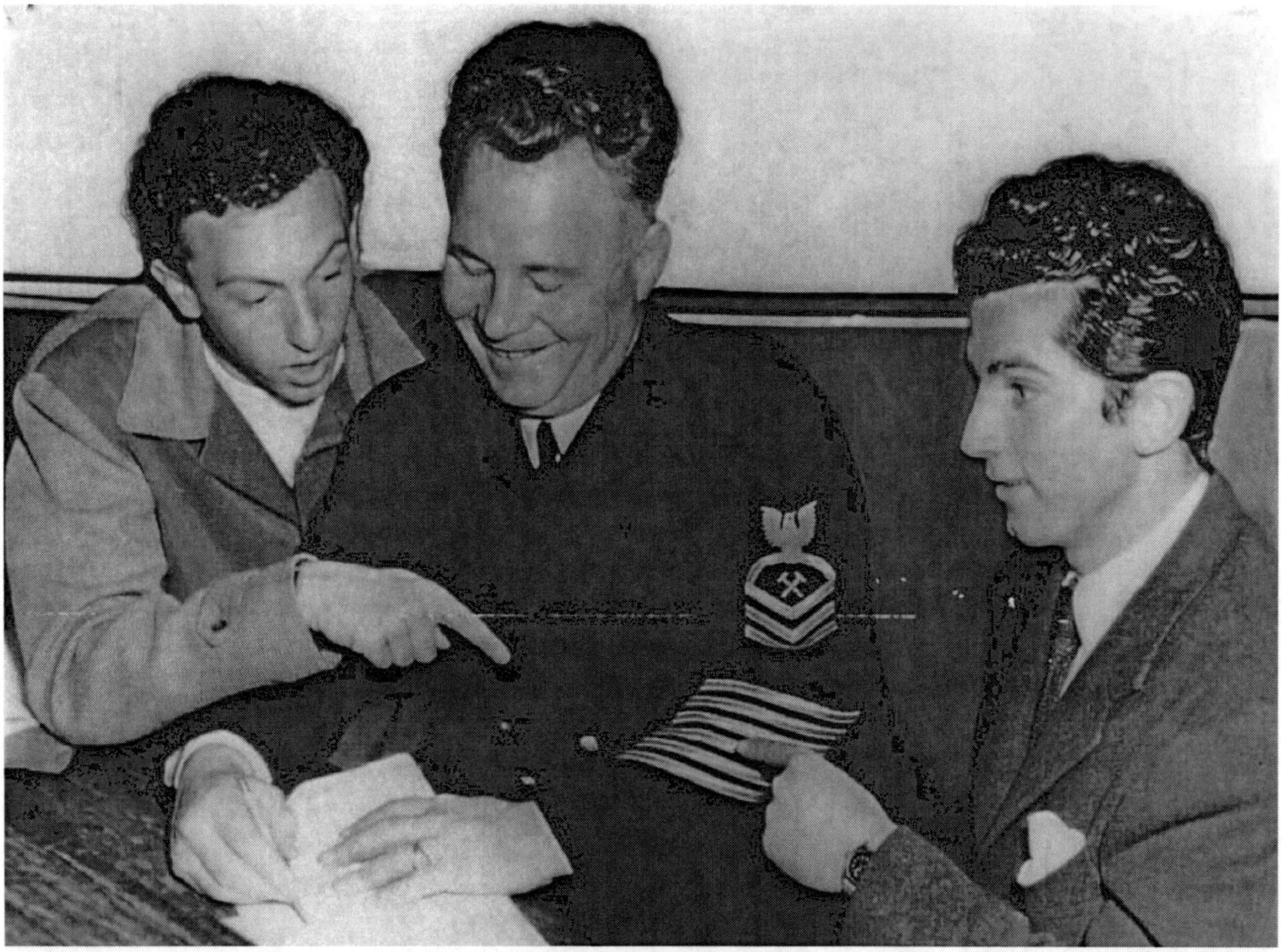

Gabe Dell joins service while Norman Abbott looks on

Gray Crosby and Huntz Hall doing a Night Club Act

Gabe Dell, sharped dressed man

Gil Stratton

Great shot of Bernard Punsly for the 1938 film Little Tough Guy

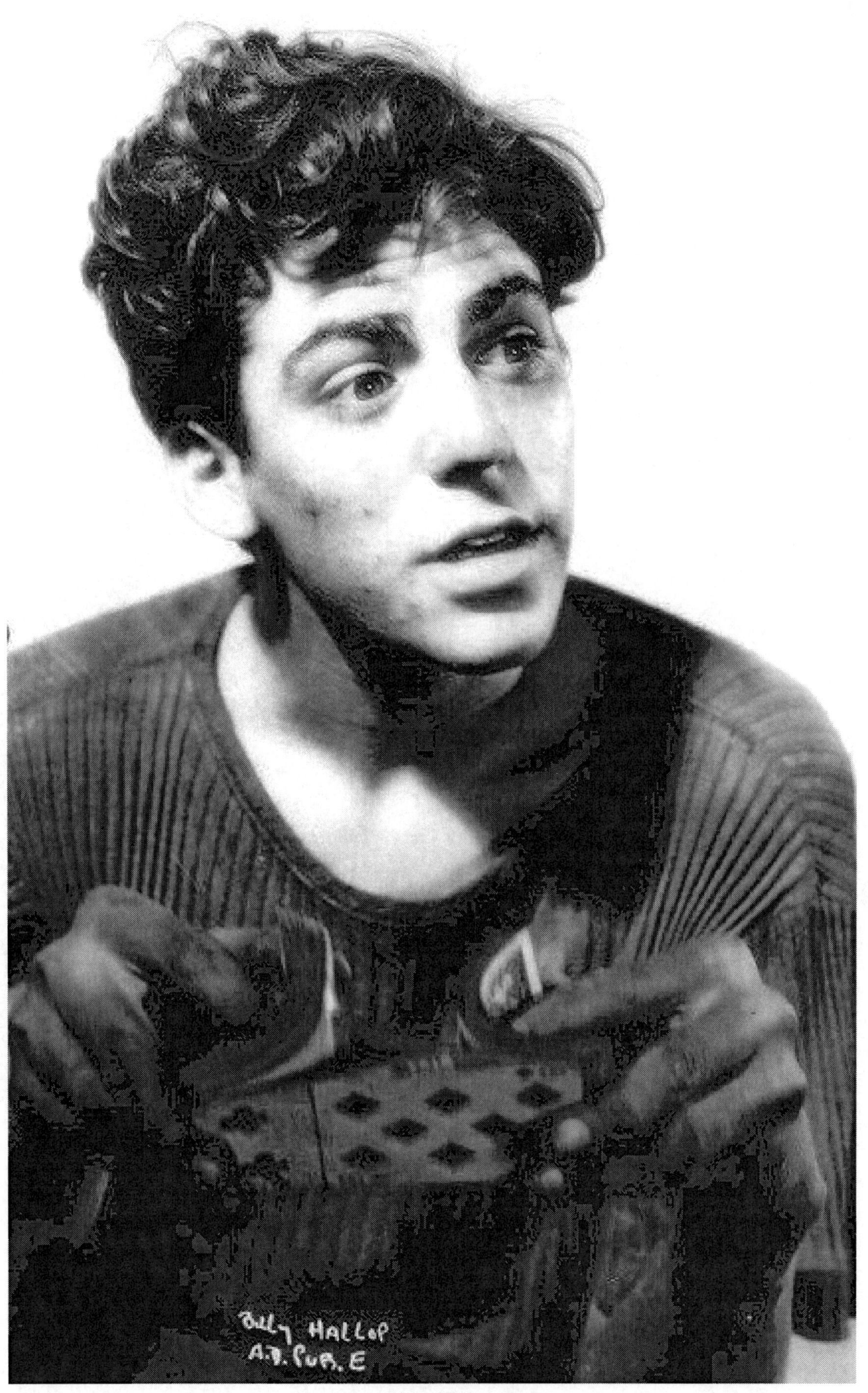

Great shot of Billy Halop

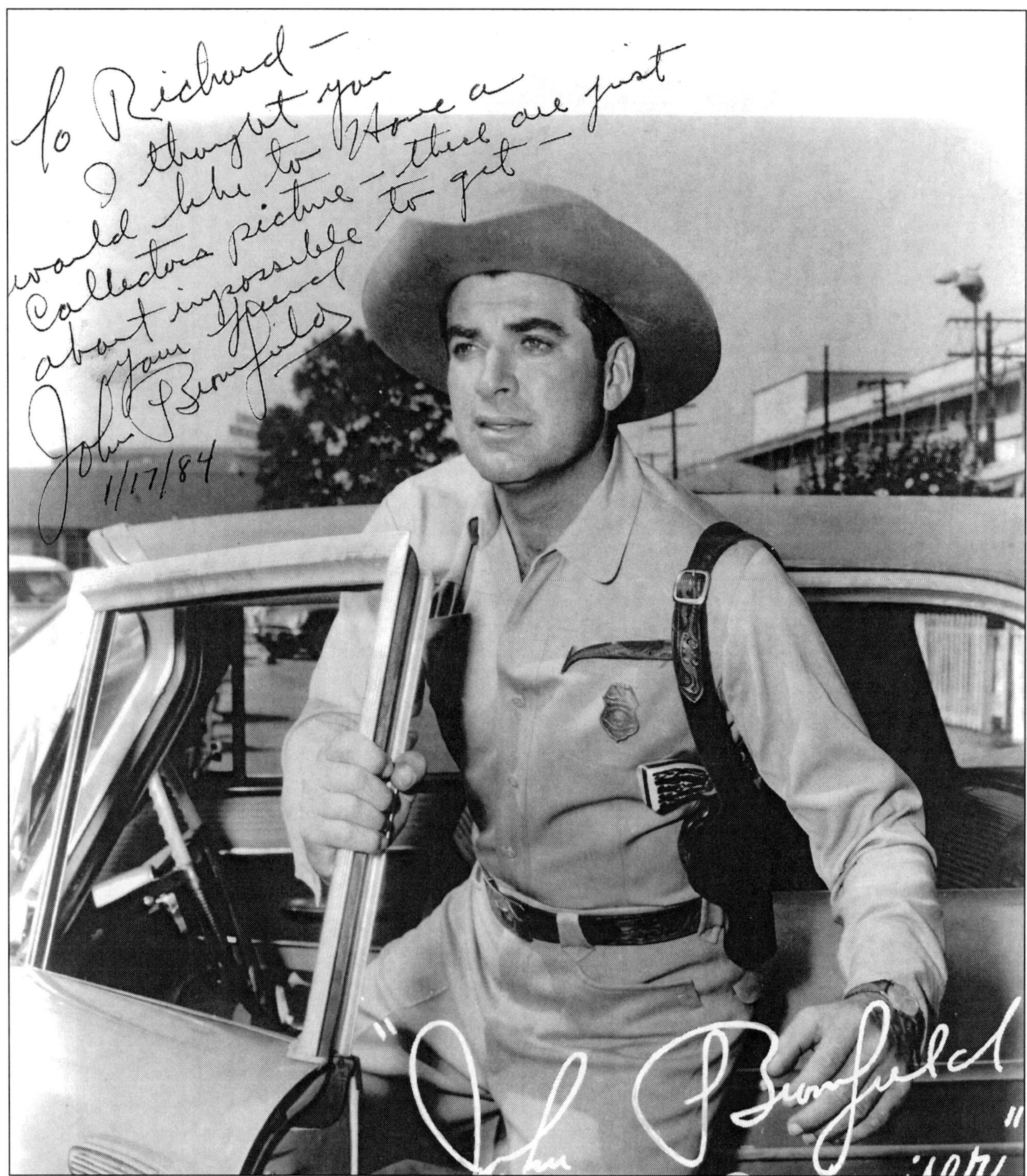

Great shot of John Bromfield who played Biff in the Bowery Boys film Hold That Line

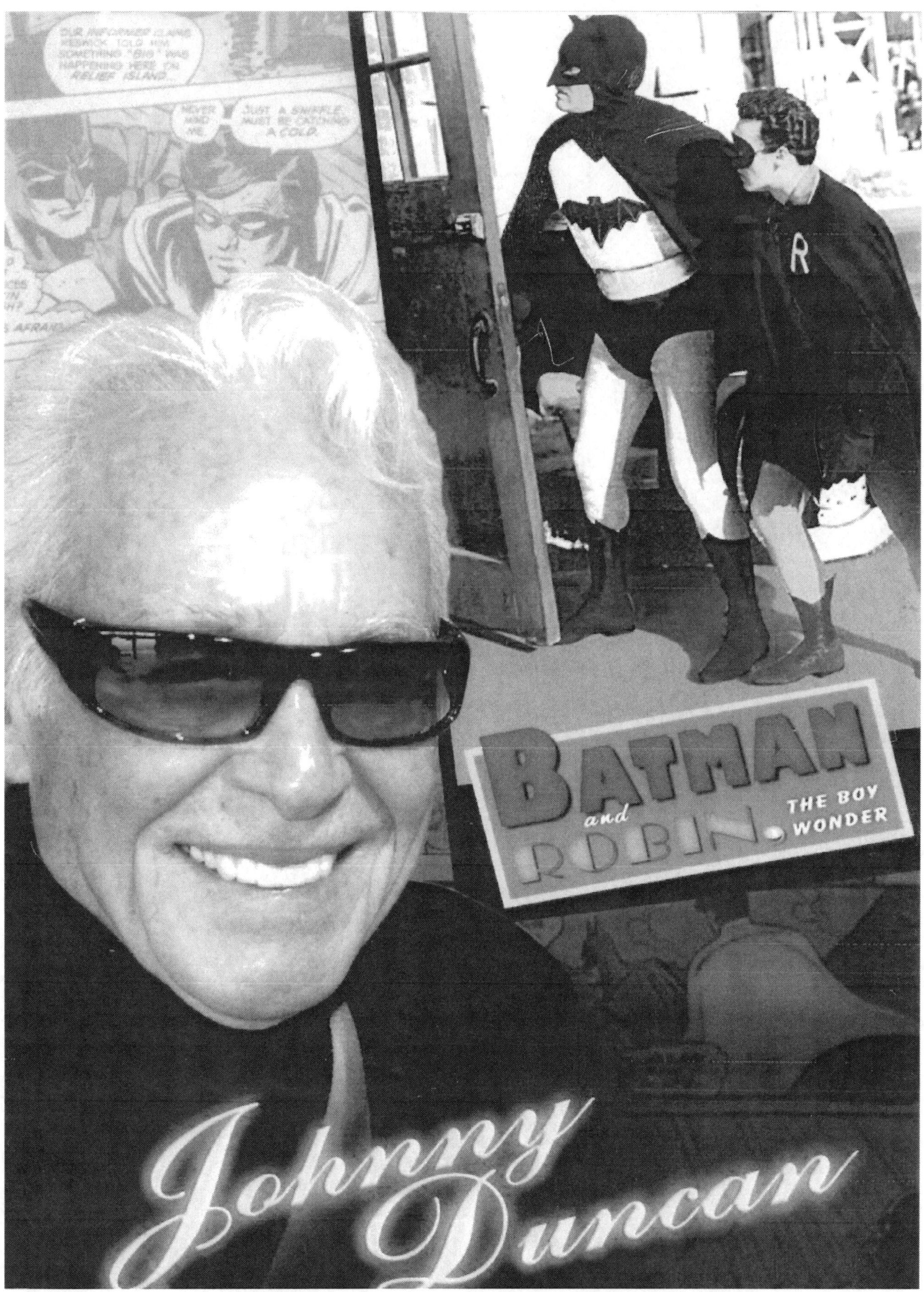

Great shot of Johnny Duncan, Robin, The Boy Wonder

Great shot of Mendie Koenig

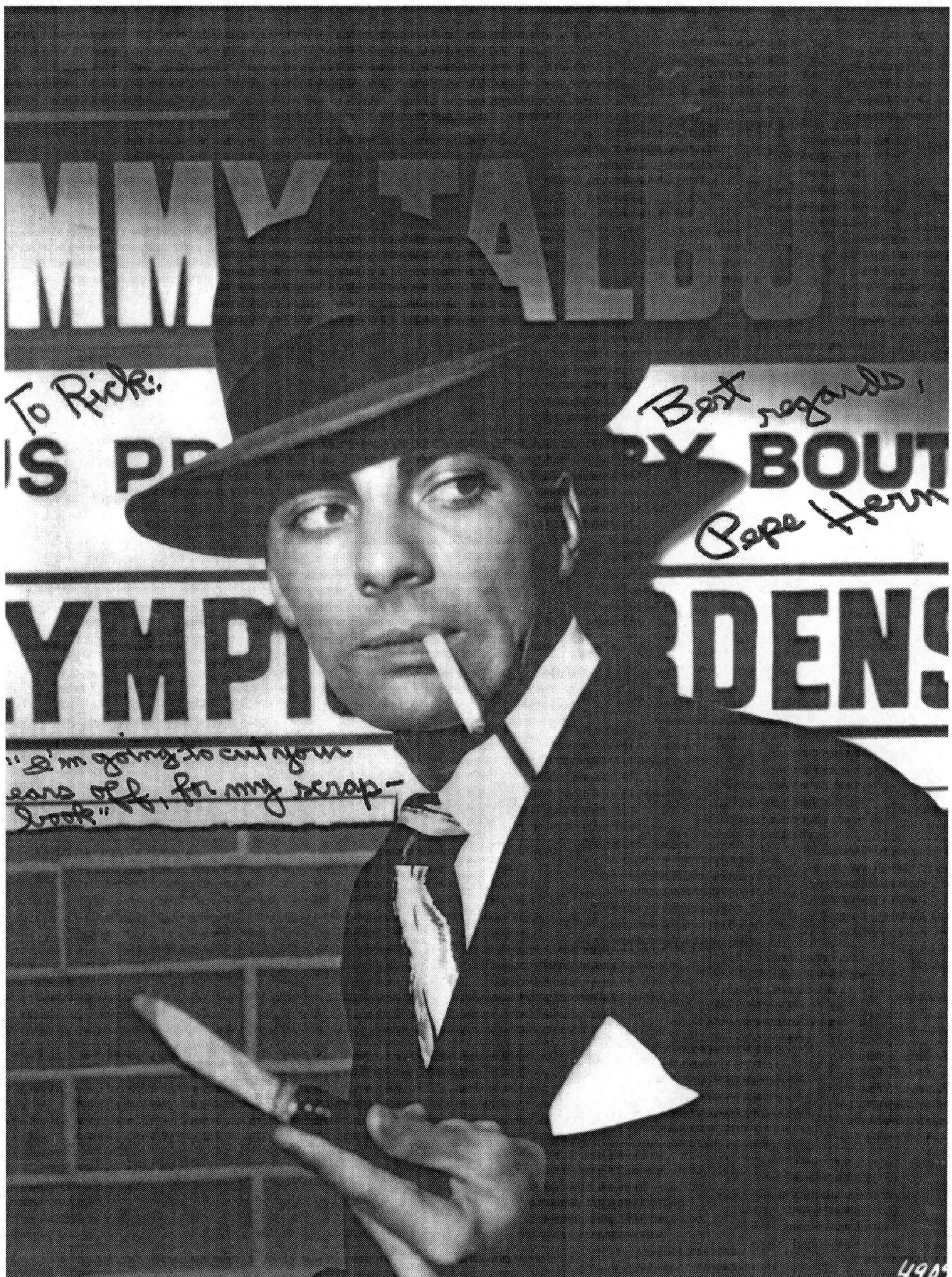

Great shot of Pepe Hern as Bertie Spangler in the film Angels in Disguise

Hall and Dell pose for this shot while doing a stage play

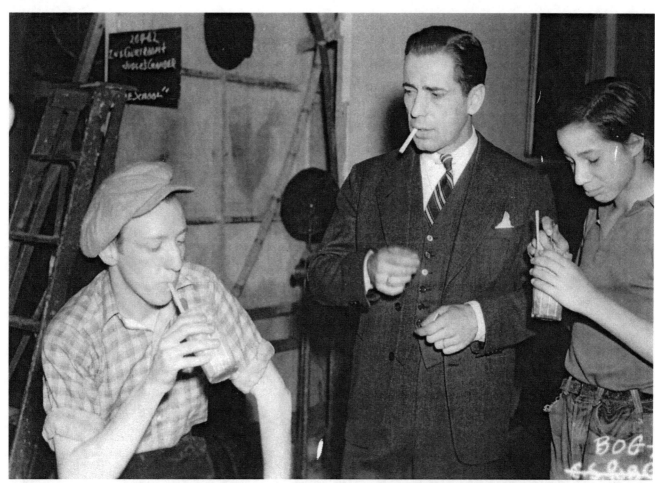

Hall and Jordan drink milk shakes with pal Bogart on the set of Crime School

Hally Chester relaxing

Hally Chester as Dopey in Little Tough Guy

Hally Chester in the film Little Tough Guy

Hally Chester, David Gorcey, Frankie Darro and Don Latorre in Juvenile Court

Halop and Hall read a telegram in this publicity still from Call a Messenger

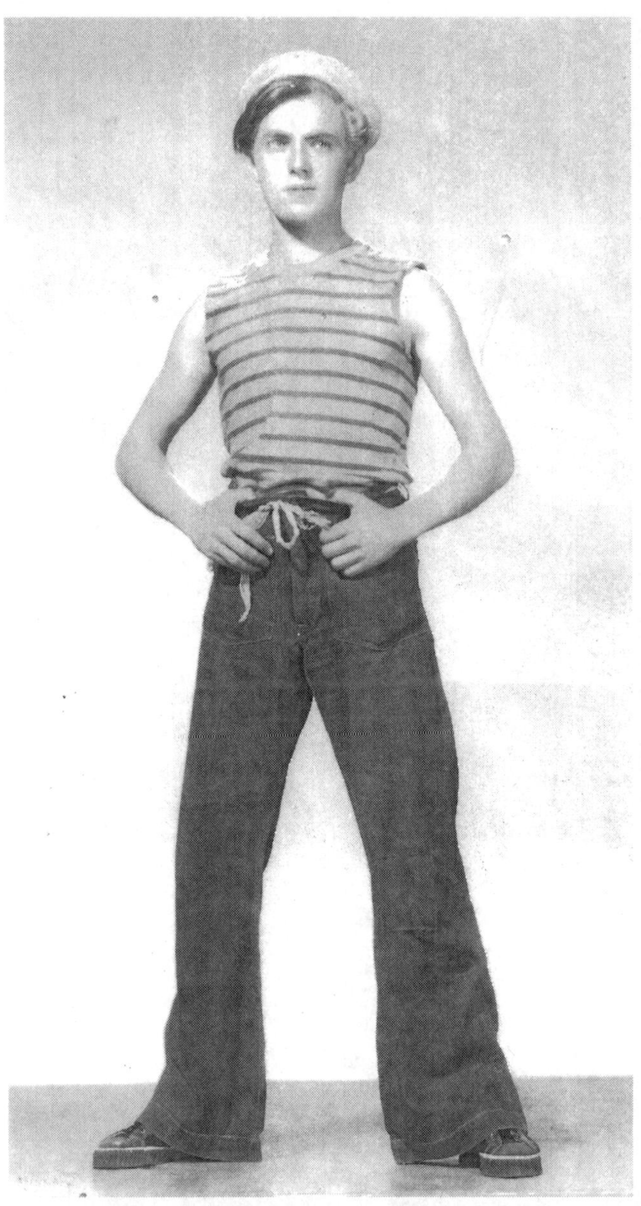

Harris Berger as Sailor in the 1938 film Little Tough Guy

Head shot of Leo Gorcey from the film Dead End

Head shot of Huntz Hall from the film Gentle Giant

Head shot of Haris Berger from the play Dead End

Head shot of Theodore Newton as Gimpty from the play Dead End

Harry Carey chats with the little tough guys, while on the set

Huntz Hall in the 1950s,and in 1967

Head shot of Buddy Gorman as Butch in the film Lets Go Navy

Head shot of Frankie Burke in his film debut in, Angels With Dirty Faces

Head shot of Huntz Hall for the film Dead End

Head shot of Jackie Cooper for the Little Tough Guy film, Newsboys Home

Head shot of Leo Gorcey from the film Dead End

Huntz Hall in all his glory as one of The Bowery Boys

Huntz Hall in Valentino as Jesse Lasky

I don't want to die

Huntz Hall, Billy Halop and Gabe Dell at the premier of the film Dead End

Huntz Hall in Wonder Man

Dead End Kids Tour With Duke: Pistol-packing Dead End Kids Huntz Hall (l.) and Gabe Dell (r.) gag with bandleader Duke Ellington during stage show at Chicago's Regal Theater. It marked the first appearance of the movie bad boys before a Negro audience.

Huntz Hall, Duke Ellington, Gabe Dell, playing at a Chicago Night Club, in front of all black audience

Huntz Hall, in all his glory

If a Dead End kid want's a kiss, he get's it,Ann Sheridan waits for the pucker

In this publicity still for the film Angels Wash Their Faces

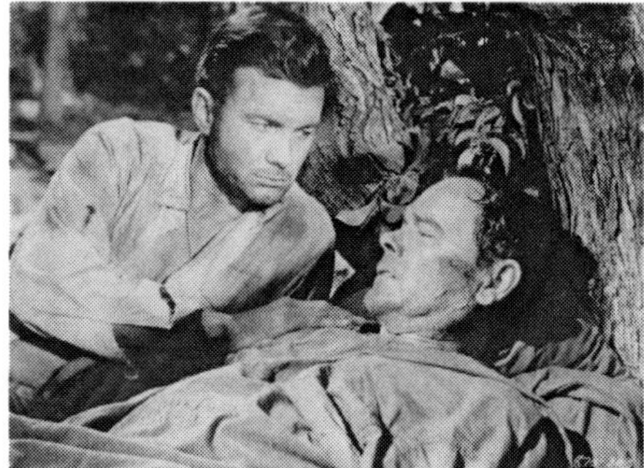

Jimmy McCallion in the film PT 109

Johnny Duncan far right in a scene from The Cain Mutiny

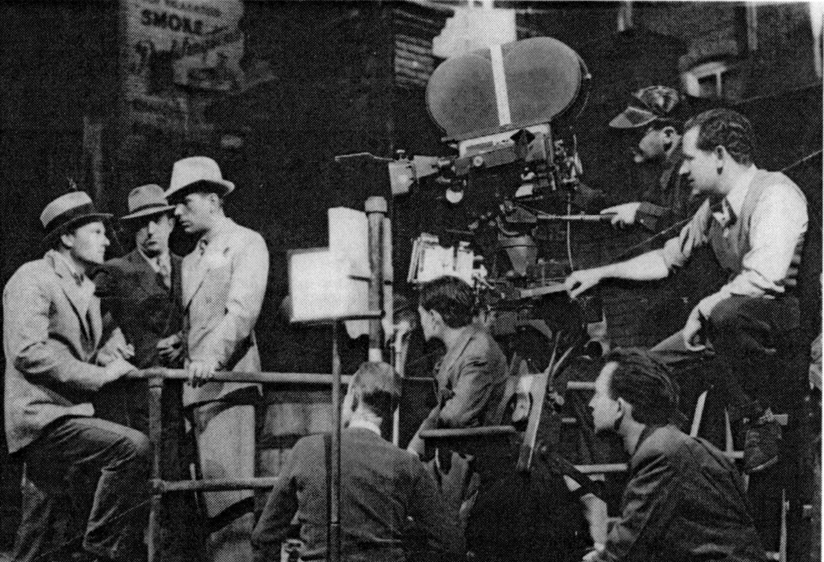

Joel McCrea and Humphrey Bogart watch director William Wyler filming a scene from Dead End

Johnny Duncan

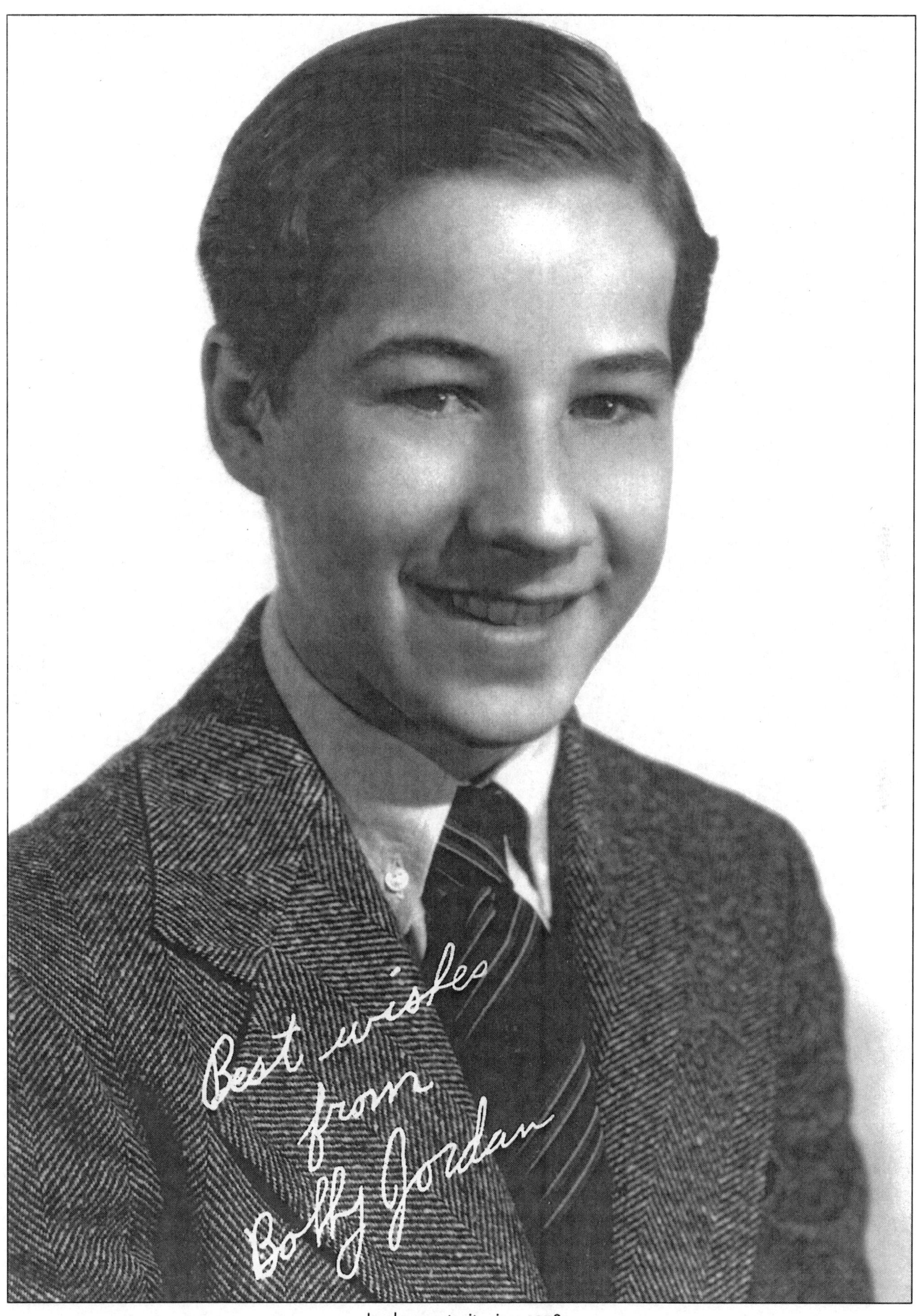
Best wishes
from
Bobby Jordan

Jordan portrait, circa 1938

Judy Garland and Bobby Jordan share some fun at the Roll Rink

Ken Howell in jr. g-men

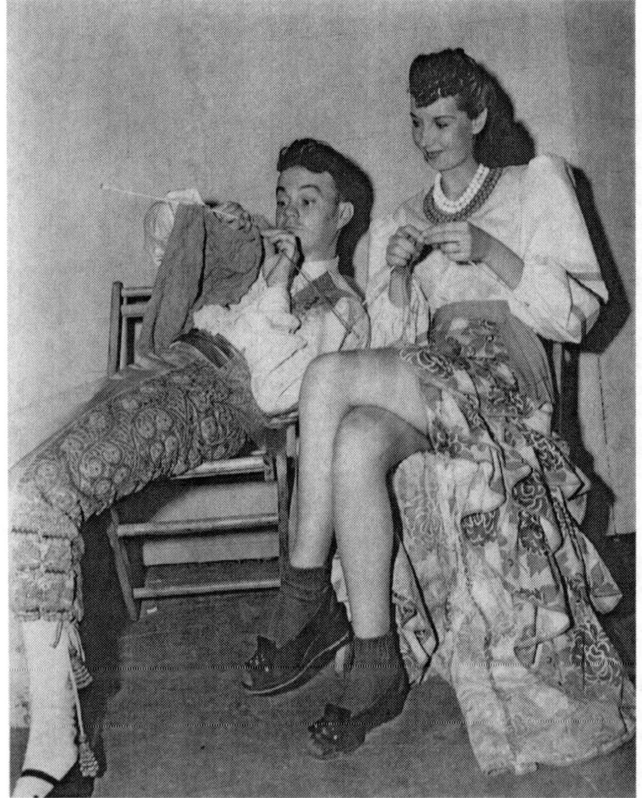

Knit 1 pearl 2, on the set of Born to Sing

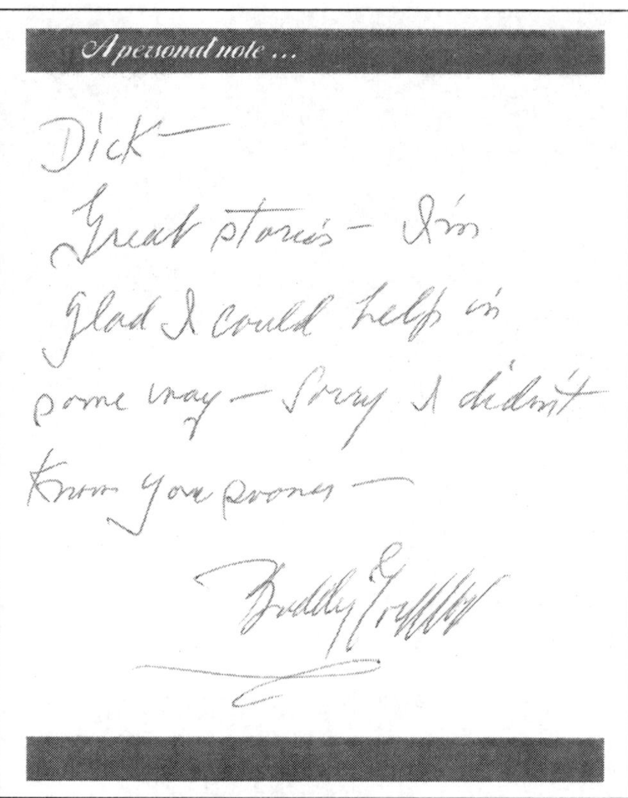

A personal note ...

Dick—

Great stories— I'm glad I could help in some way— Sorry I didn't know you sooner—

Buddy Gorman

Last letter wrote by Buddy Gorman, he passed away 9 days later

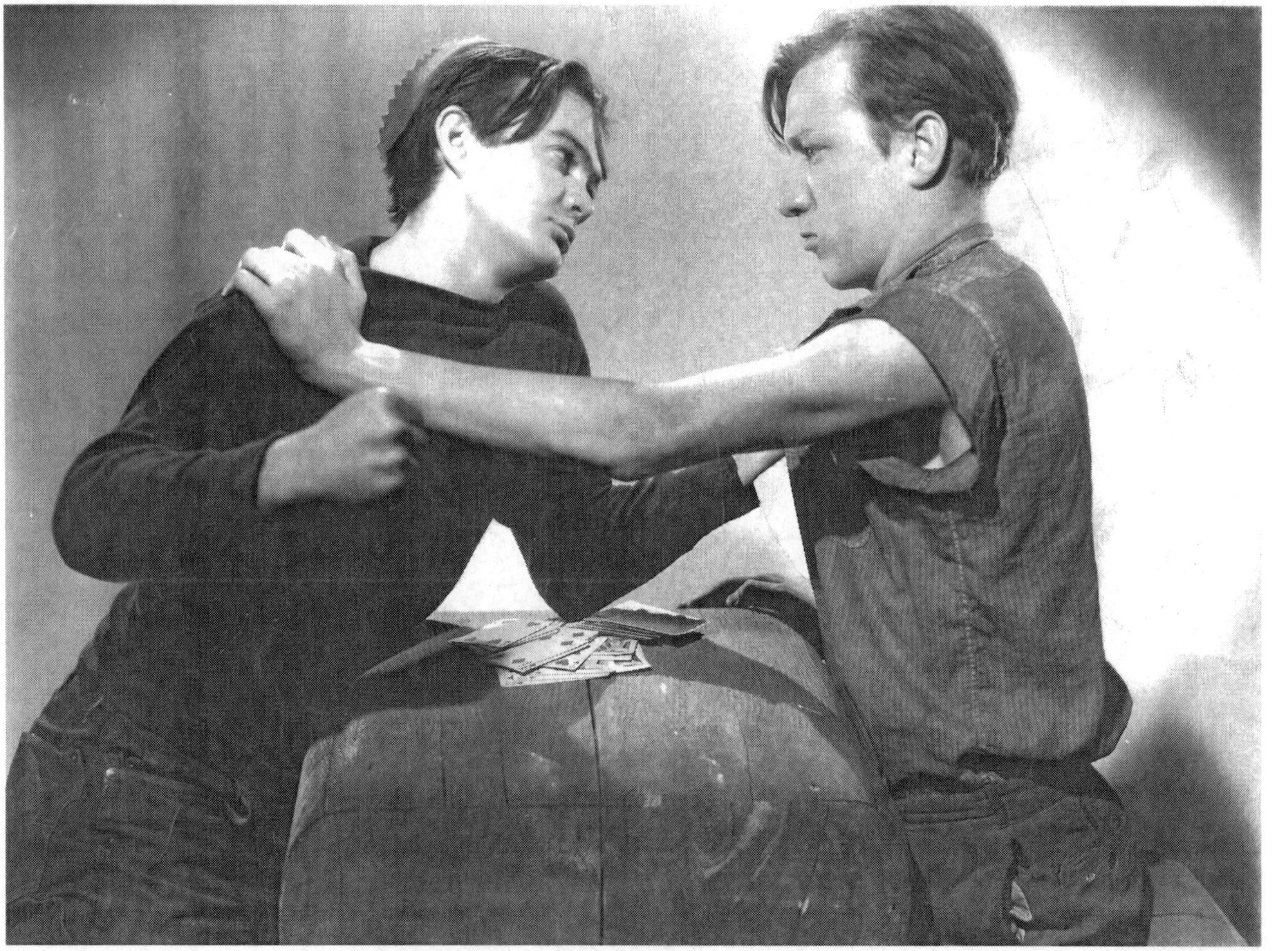

Leo Gorcey and Huntz Hall in the film Dead End

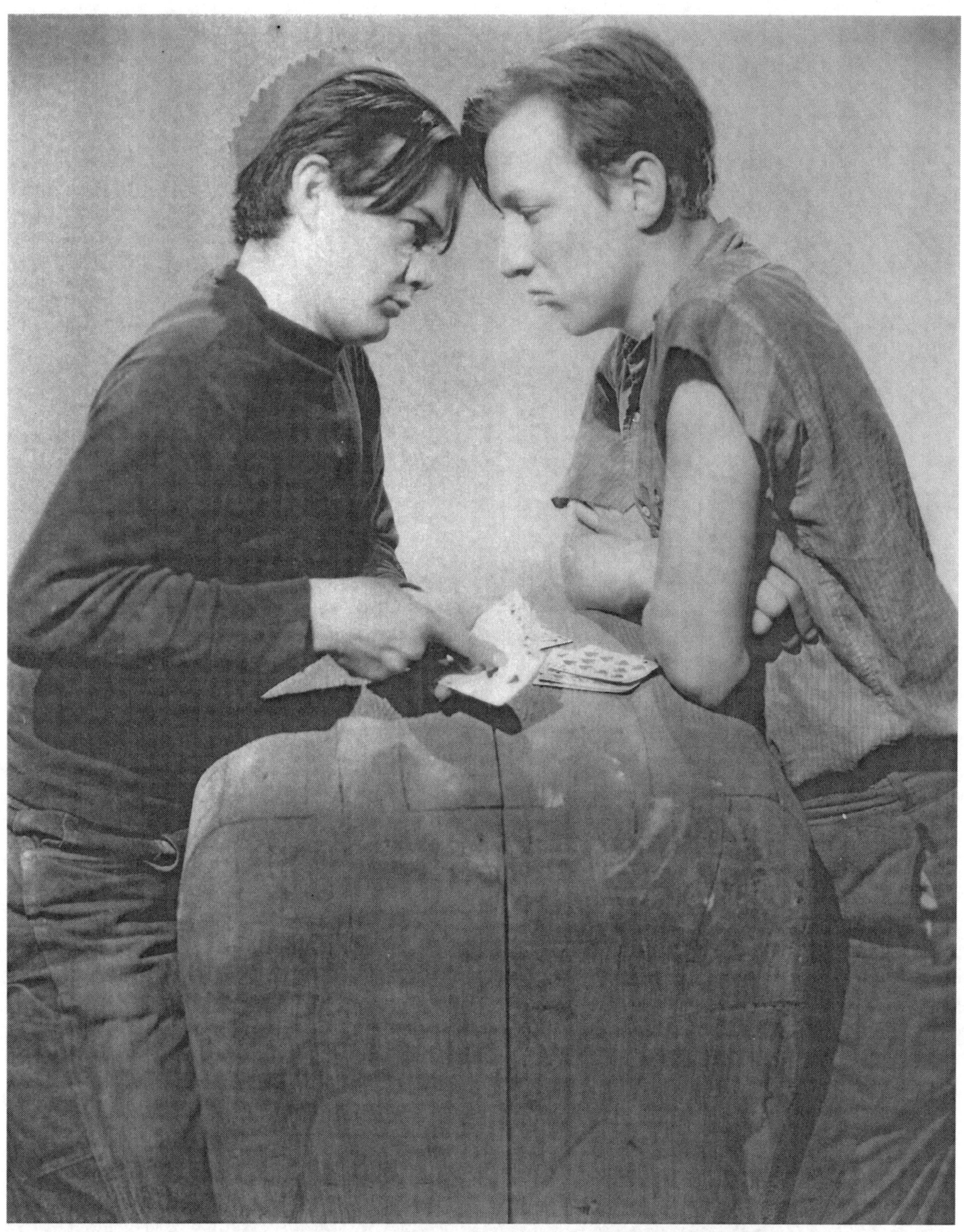

Leo Gorcey and Huntz Hall in this set up shot for the 1937 film Dead End

Leo Gorcey as Spit

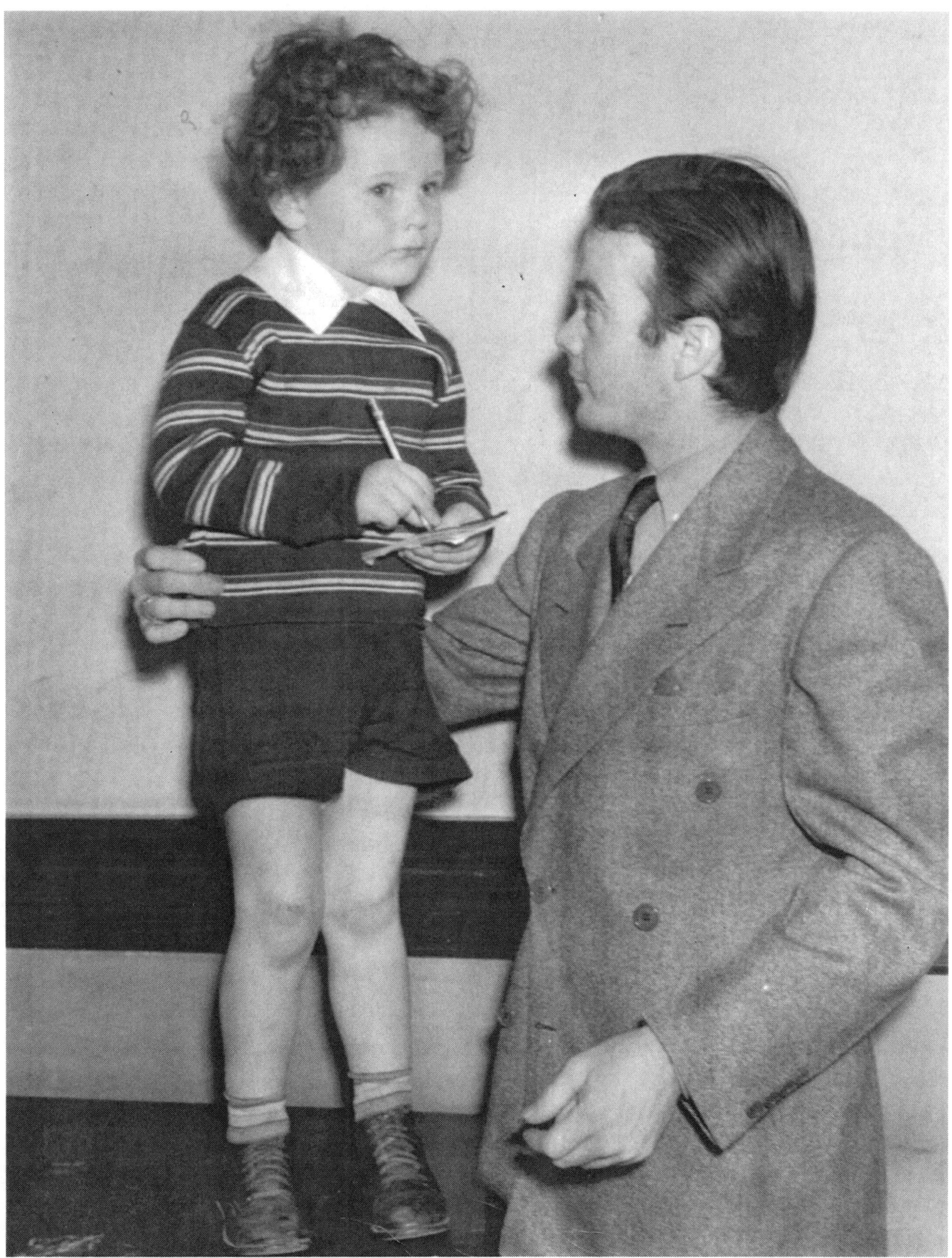

Leo Gorcey holds his little cousin, Michael J. Berry Jr. outside a court room

Leo Gorcey in a scene from the film Headin' East

Leo Gorcey is tough as nails in his role of Spike in the film Crime School

Leo Gorcey in the film Midnight Manhunt as Clutch Tracy

Leo Gorcey in Hell's Kitchen

Leo Gorcey in the film, Midnight Manhunt

Leo Gorcey on NBC radio

Leo Gorcey plays Sailor Sarecky in Destroyer, Columbia Pictures

Leo Gorcey is up to no good, in this portrait from the film Dead End

Leo Gorcey learns, knit 1 and pearl 2 from Ann Sheridan on the set

Leo Gorcey portrait from the 1938 film Crime School

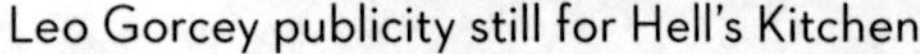

Leo Gorcey publicity still for Hell's Kitchen

Leo Gorcey with a mustache

Leo Gorcey, standing outside marriage bureau answering questions from reporters

Leo Grocey half hardly cracks a smile

Made up shot of Leo Gorcey from the 1939 film They Made Me a Criminal

Lobby card for the film Off the Record

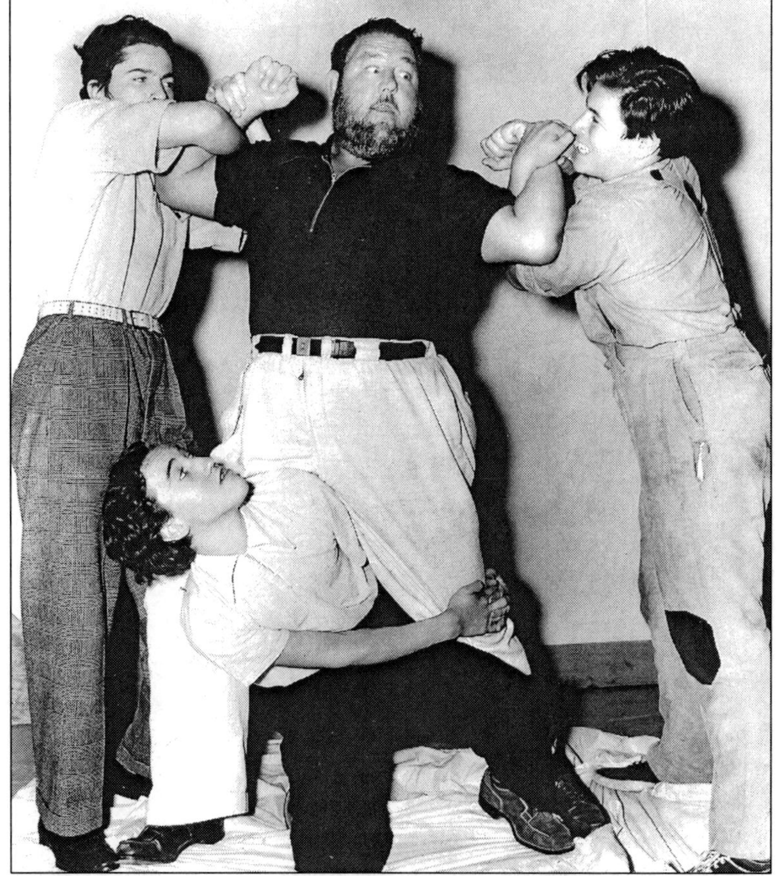

Man Mountain Dean doesn't who's he messing with, when a pays a visit to the Dead End Kids

20 July 1976

Mr. Richard Roat, Jr.
9826 South Normandy
Oaklawn, Illinois 60453

Dear Mr. Roat;

I've just received your very kind letter to Mr. Hall and without further ado; thought it best that I answer for him at this juncture.

Mr. Hall is in London, England at the present time. They will commence shooting on the film "VALENTINO" within the next few weeks. And for all intents and purposes will be locationing in various parts of the European continent; consequently, we doubt seriously the viability of a release on the picture until sometime in 1977.

I, personally would like to thank you for the poster you sent of Huntz and Gabriel Dell. It was a rather pleasant surprise to be added to the very few that Mr. Hall has been fortunate enough to keep lo these many years.

For myself, and Huntz, I would like to thank you for all the lovely correspondence we've received from you. But more importantly, for the loyalty you've shown Huntz.

I too am more than just a little impressed with the fact that you've managed to find a "fan club card" and am even more than just a little delighted at the thought of your starting a fan club for him at this time of his life. I certainly hope this can be attained.

Inasmuch as I shall be joining Mr. Hall in London on Saturday, I shall certainly bring your letter along to show him. Because his schedule will be rather tight from hereon in, I'm sure you can understand my writing.

If there is any other information you might require as regards Huntz; please fee free to contact his public relations office. They will be more than happy to aid you/

CORDIALLY,

Lee Hall

(MRS.) HUNTZ HALL

PUBLIC RELATIONS
PHIL STRASSBERG
5151 Woodman
Sherman Oaks, Calif.
914
91423

Letter from Huntz Hall's Wife-Lee

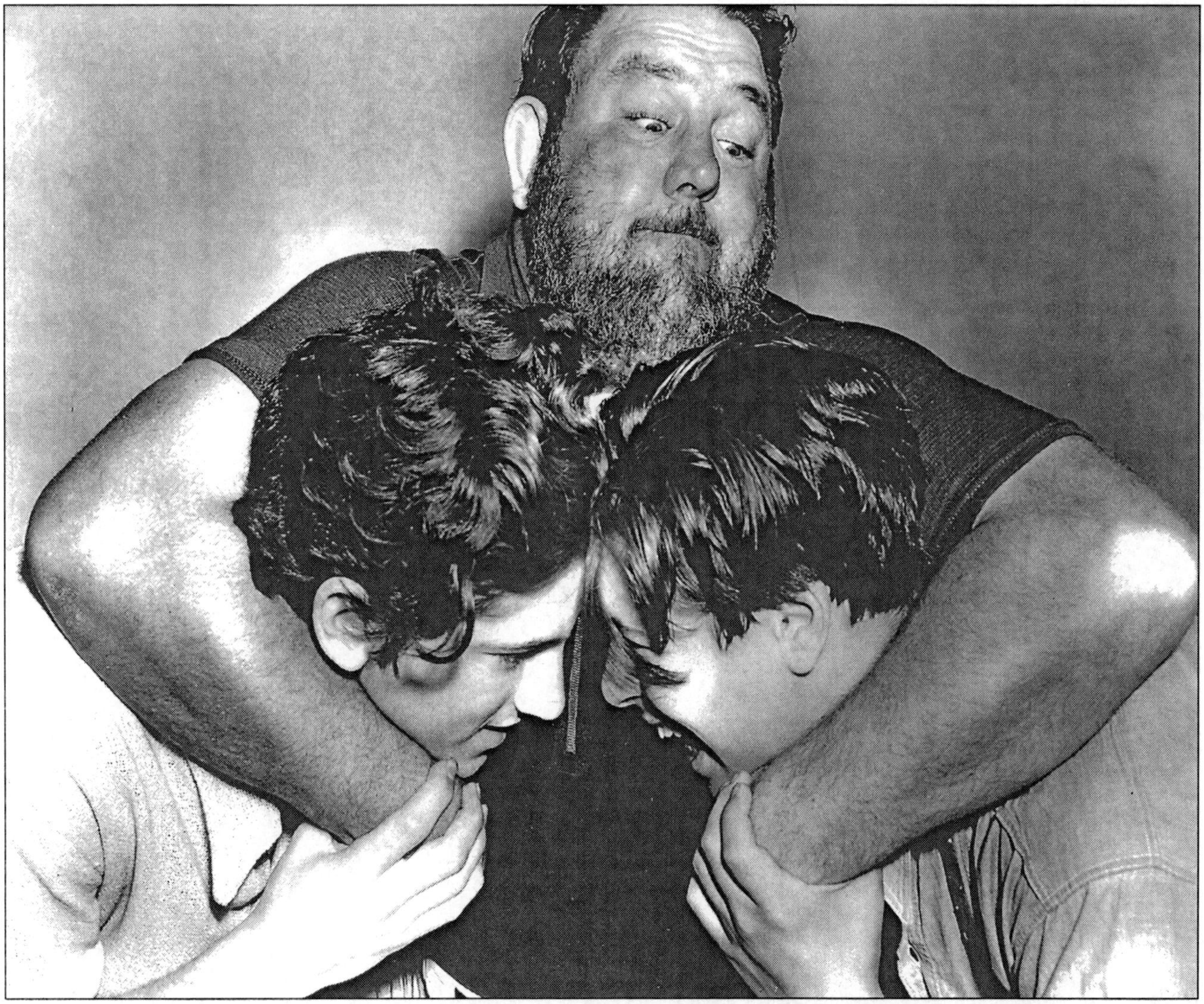

Man Mountain Dean pays a visit to Gabe Dell and Bernard Punsly

Mendie Koenig (for ground) dancing in the play-The Time of my Life

Mendie Koenig and author, August, 2012

Mendie Koenig and my daughter Jennny, August 2012

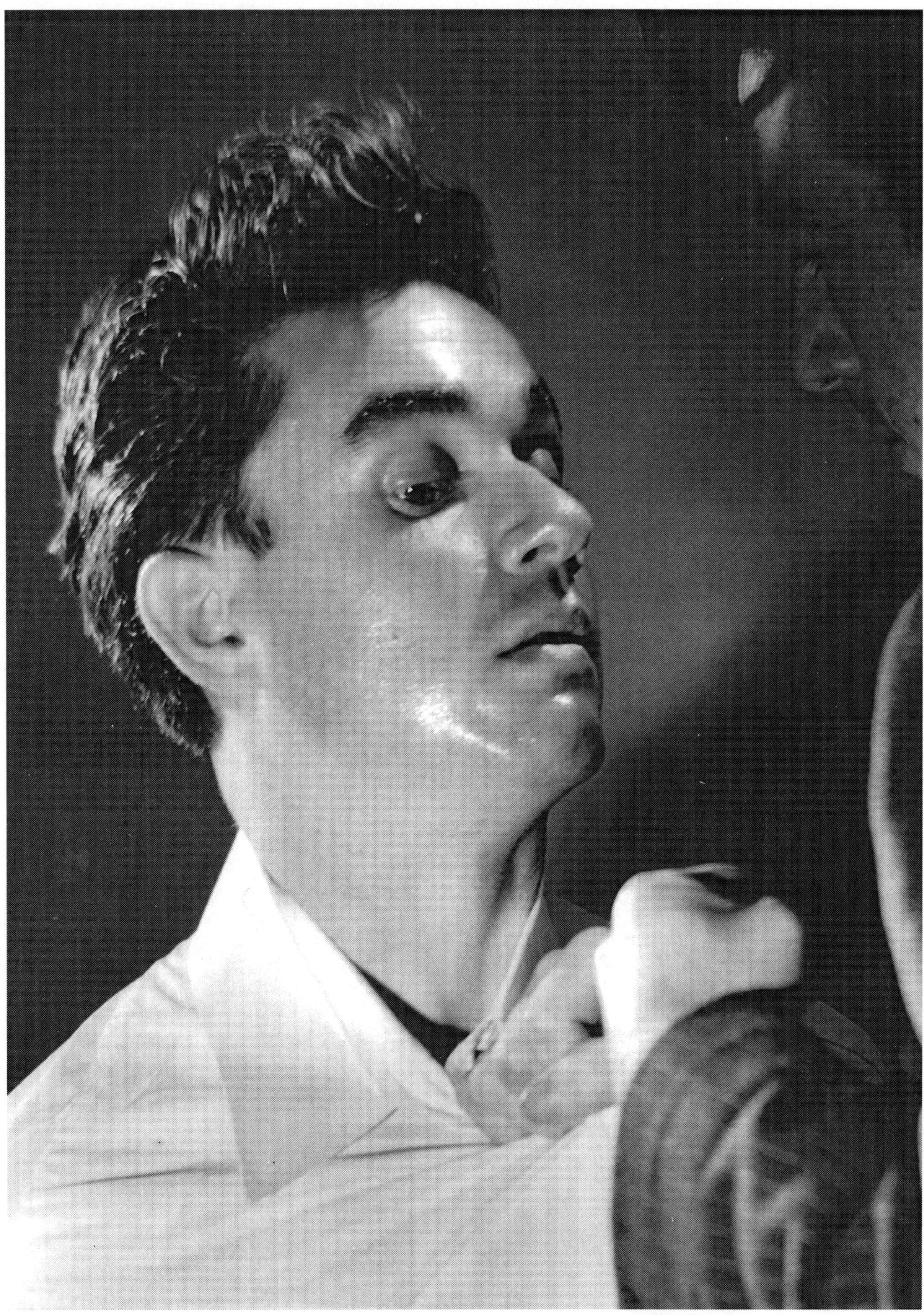

Mendie Koenig plays a tough guy with Lash La Rue in this scene

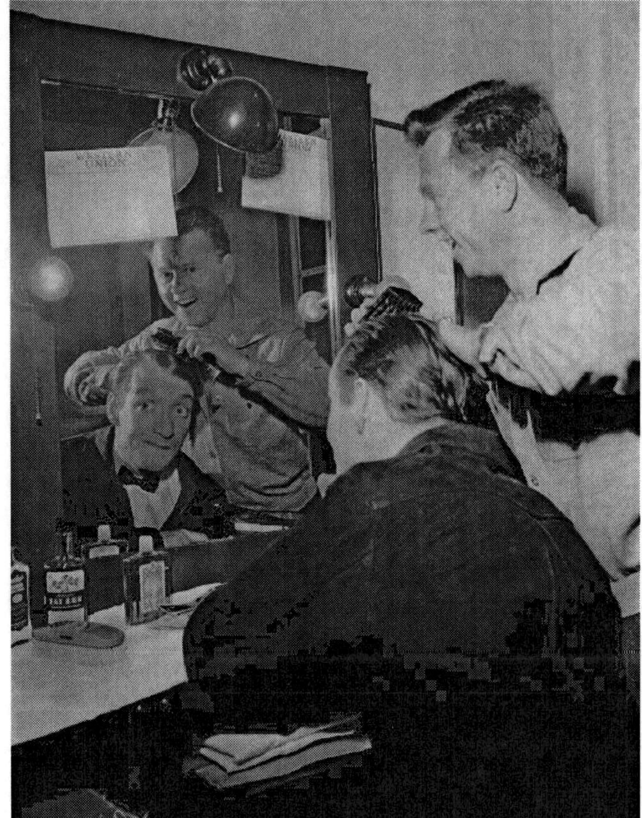

Mickey Rooney, Huntz Hall, 1951 Girl Crazy

Nice shot of Leo Gorcey looking perplexed

Newly Married Leo and his bride share a bite

Norman Abbott

One shot Al Stone

Nice shot of Huntz Hall from the 1940s film Give Us Wings

NBC Television

NBC TELEVISION CAPTION
SUBJECT: (l. to r.) Norman Abbott, Helen Woods and Gabe Dell
PROGRAM: "BROADWAY OPEN HOUSE" (Monday and Wednesdays)
BROADCAST: NBC-TV, Monday and Wednesday, 11:00 p.m., EST).

Norman Abbott, Helen Woods and Gabe Dell, Broadway Open House photo

One sheet poster for the Huntz Hall film College Days

One shot Bill Bates, aka-Sleepy Dave

One shot Eddie Mills

One time Bowery Boy William Frambes in the film Nothing But Trouble

One shot Leo Borden

Original cap-A Matinee Idol with a cast iron chin, shot of Charles Duncan

Original cap-Frankie Burke visits with Hollywood make up artist Wally Westmore

Original cap-He Had To Be Tough, Billy Benedict in Little Tough Guys in Society

Original cap-Top, Lester Jay, David Gorcey and Hally Chester with Maxie Rosenbloom

Original caption-The Plagues of Burbank, Michael Curtiz didn't know if he was filming Angels or six Nuts

Cap-Original caption reads-Dressed To Kill

Top, Frankie Thomas, Hally Chester and Billy Benedict in the film Little Tough Guys in Society

Top, Charles Duncan, David Gorcey and Harris Berger in this publicity still from Little Tough Guys in Society

Original caption-Slapsie Maxie Rosenbloom pugilist tries to get a hold of one of the Little Tough Guys

Pictured here with W.C. Fields is Bernard Punsly in this scene from The Big Broadcast of 1938

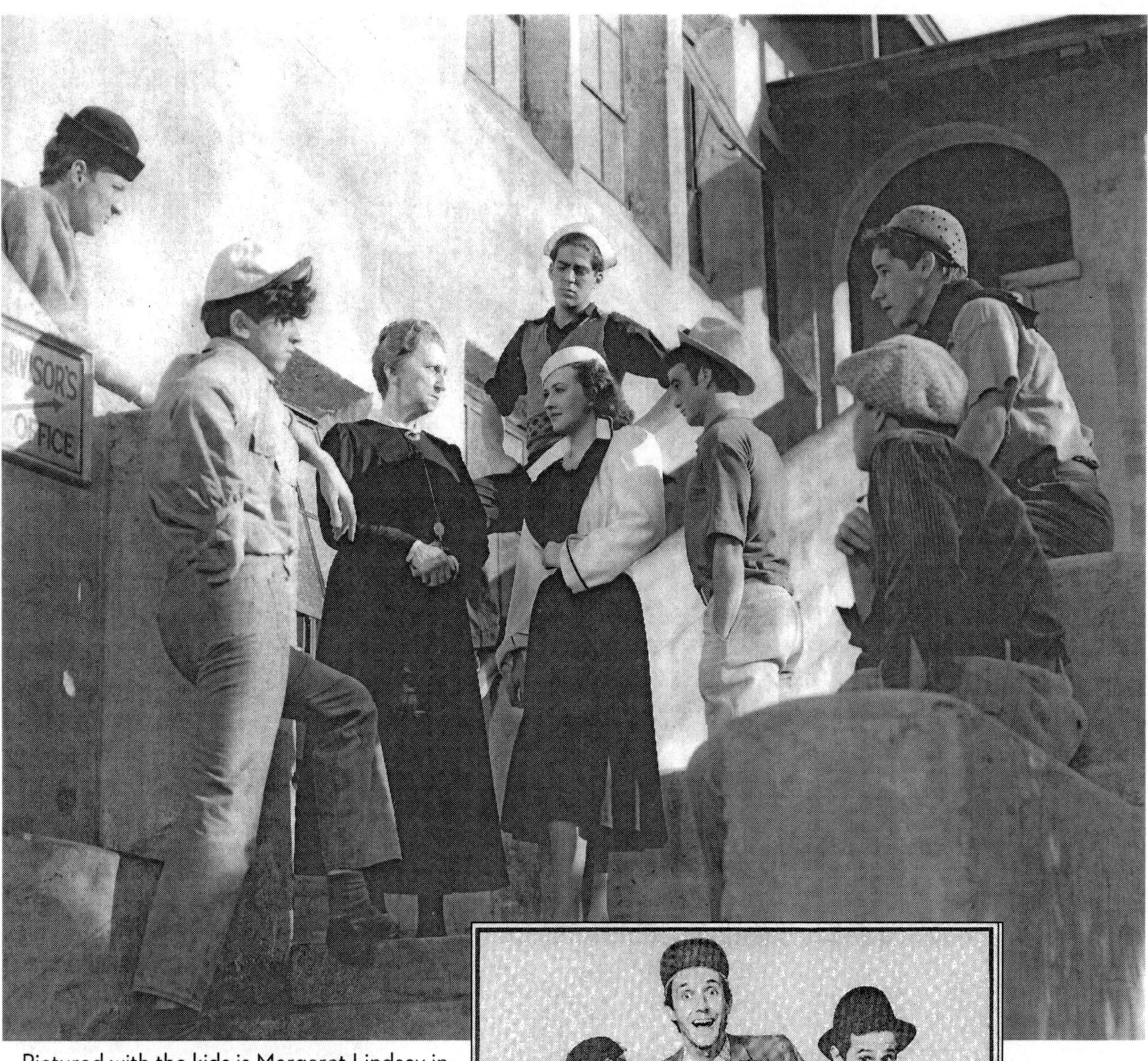

Pictured with the kids is Margaret Lindsay in this scene from Hell's Kitchen

Play bill from the play The Dead End Kid

One Act Theatre Company Presents
the world premiere of

THE DEAD END
K I D

by MICHAEL LYNCH a new musical from the award-winning
SAN JOAQUIN BLUES team!
Music by STEVE SIGEL and ANDY KULBERG
Lyrics by STEVE SIGEL
Choreography by RODGER HENDERSON
Directed by SIMON L. LEVY

Portrait still of Paul Nichols from the Bobby Jordan film Reformatory

Portrait of Bernard Punsly from the film Dead End

Portrait of Bobby Jordan from the film Dead End (1937)

Portrait of Bobby Jordan from the film Give Us Wings

Portrait of Bobby Jordan

Portrait of Bobby Stone as one of the East Side Kids

Portrait of Billy Halop-Cold Killer

Portrait of George Offerman

Portrait of Hally Chester as Dopey in Little Tough Guy

Portrait of Stanley Clements for his role in Racing Luck

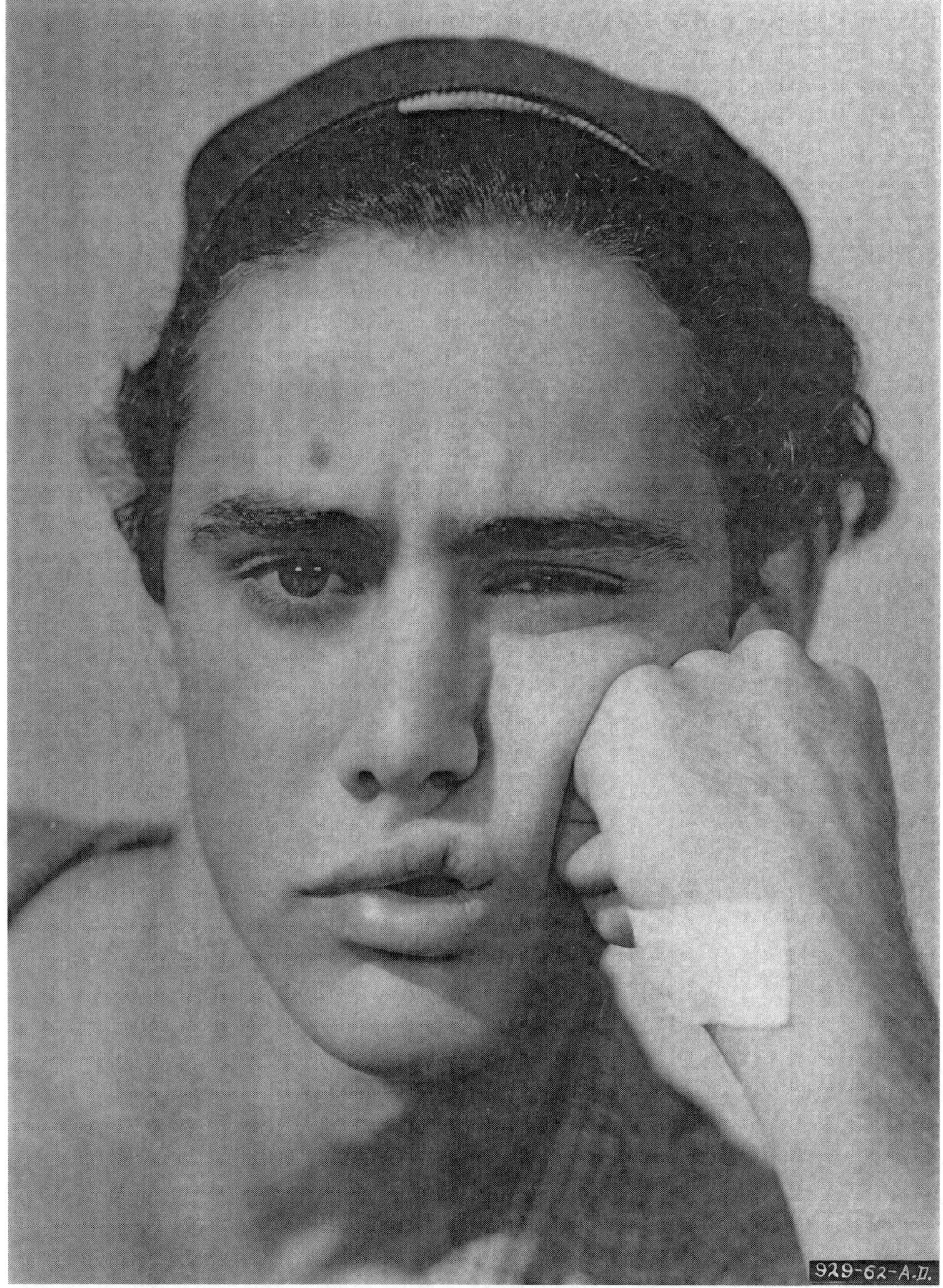

Portrait shot of David Gorcey for the film Little Tough Guy

Portrait shot of Donald Haines

Portrait shot of Leo Gorcey promoting his stint on the Bob Hope Show

Portrait still of Huntz, 1938

Portrait still of Bill Chaney

Portrait still of David Gorcey for the film Little Tough Guy

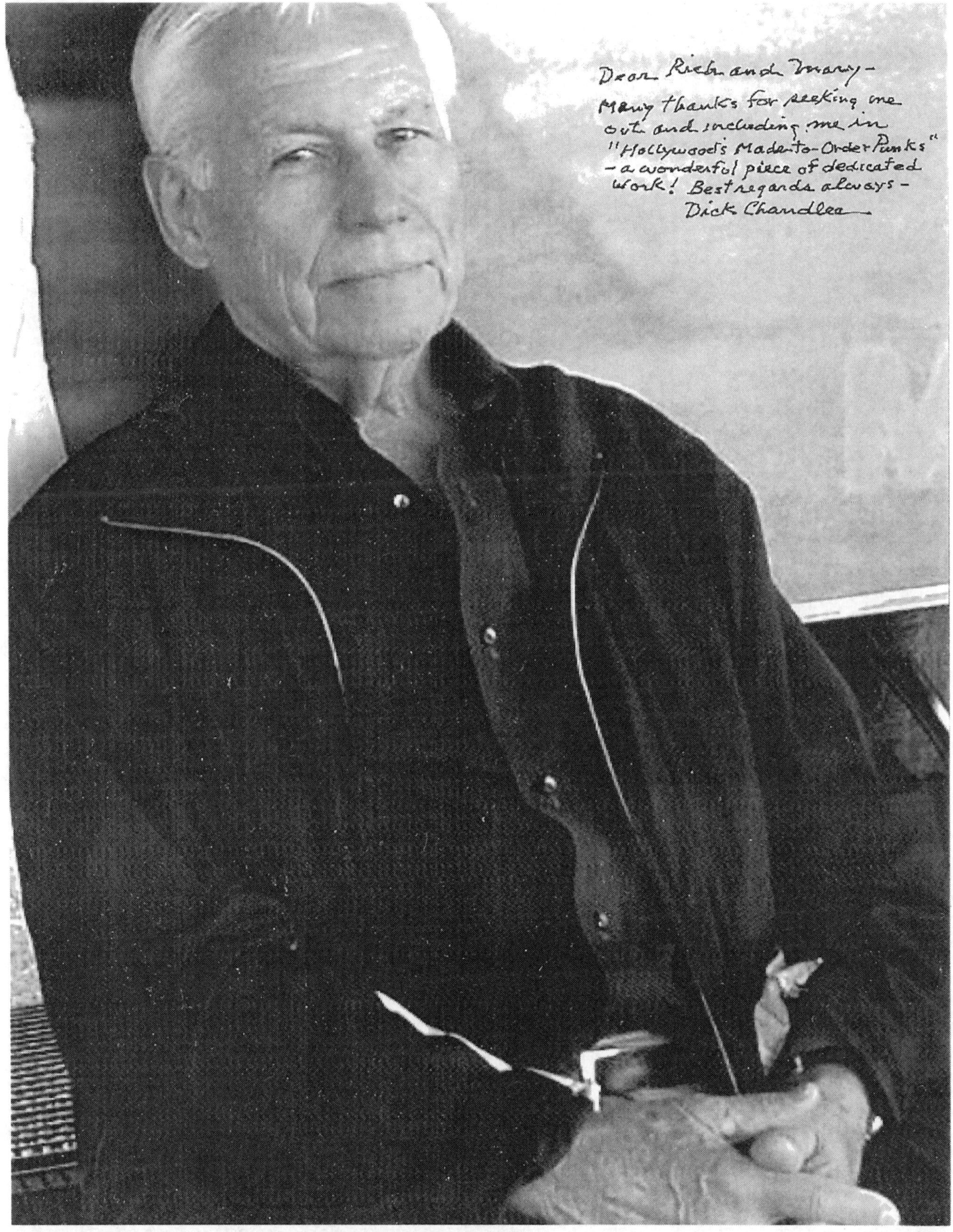

Dear Rich and Mary-
Many thanks for seeking me out and including me in "Hollywood's Made-to-Order Punks" - a wonderful piece of dedicated work! Best regards always -
Dick Chandlee

Portrait still of Dick Chandlee, (Central casting is calling)

To Paul
Atticus' best
Product
Best Wishes
Gene
5/37

Portrait still of Eugene Francis, from May, 1937

Portrait still of Frank Jr. Coghlan

Portrait still of Frankie Burke for the film, You Can't Get Away with Murder

Portrait still of Gabe Dell for the film Crime School

Portrait still of Huntz Hall from, Hit The Road, 1941

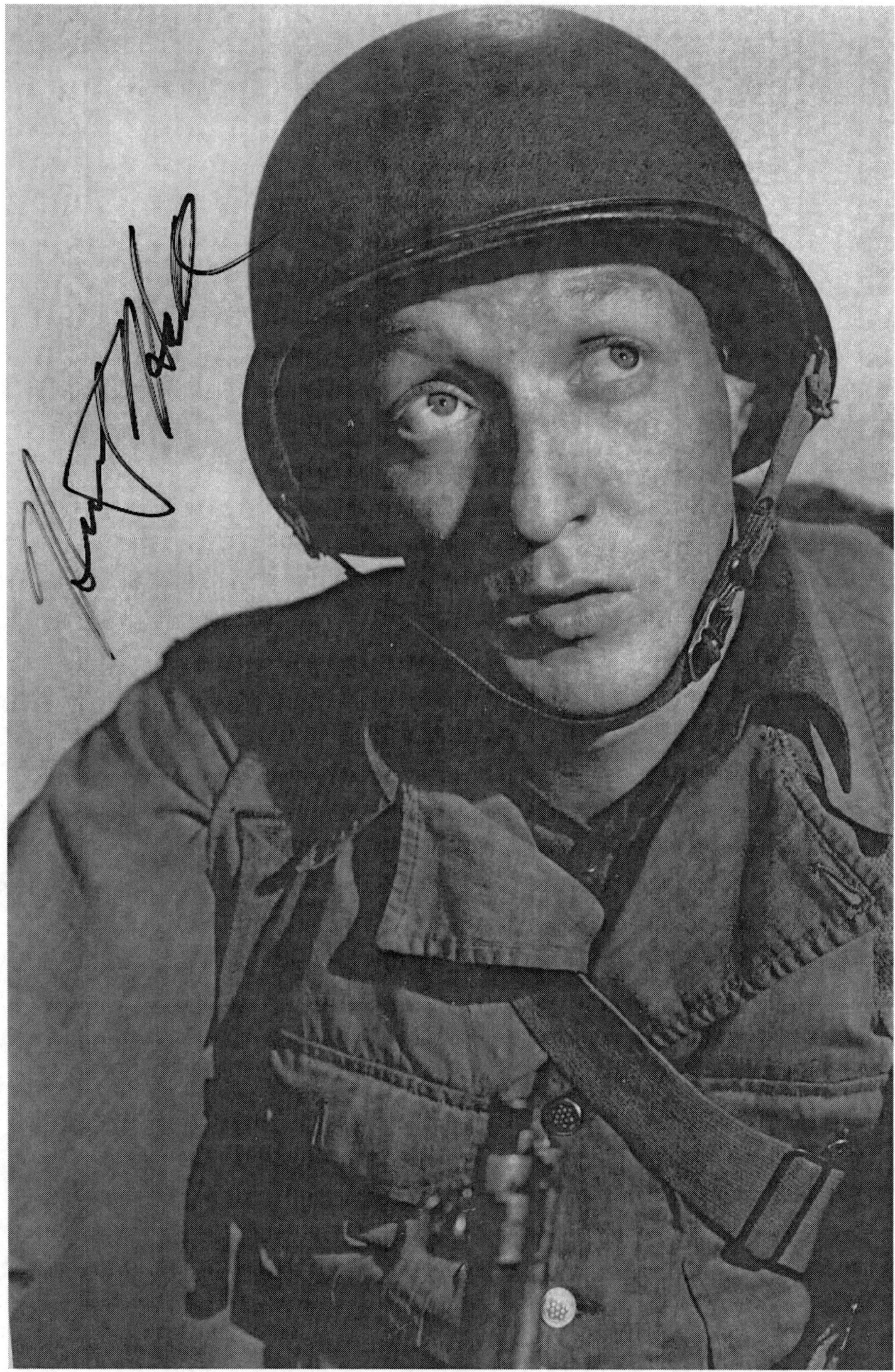

Portrait still of Huntz Hall in the film A Walk In The Sun

Portrait still of Huntz Hall

Portrait still of Jack Edwards

Portrait still of Jackie Searl

Portrait still of Jimmy McCallion

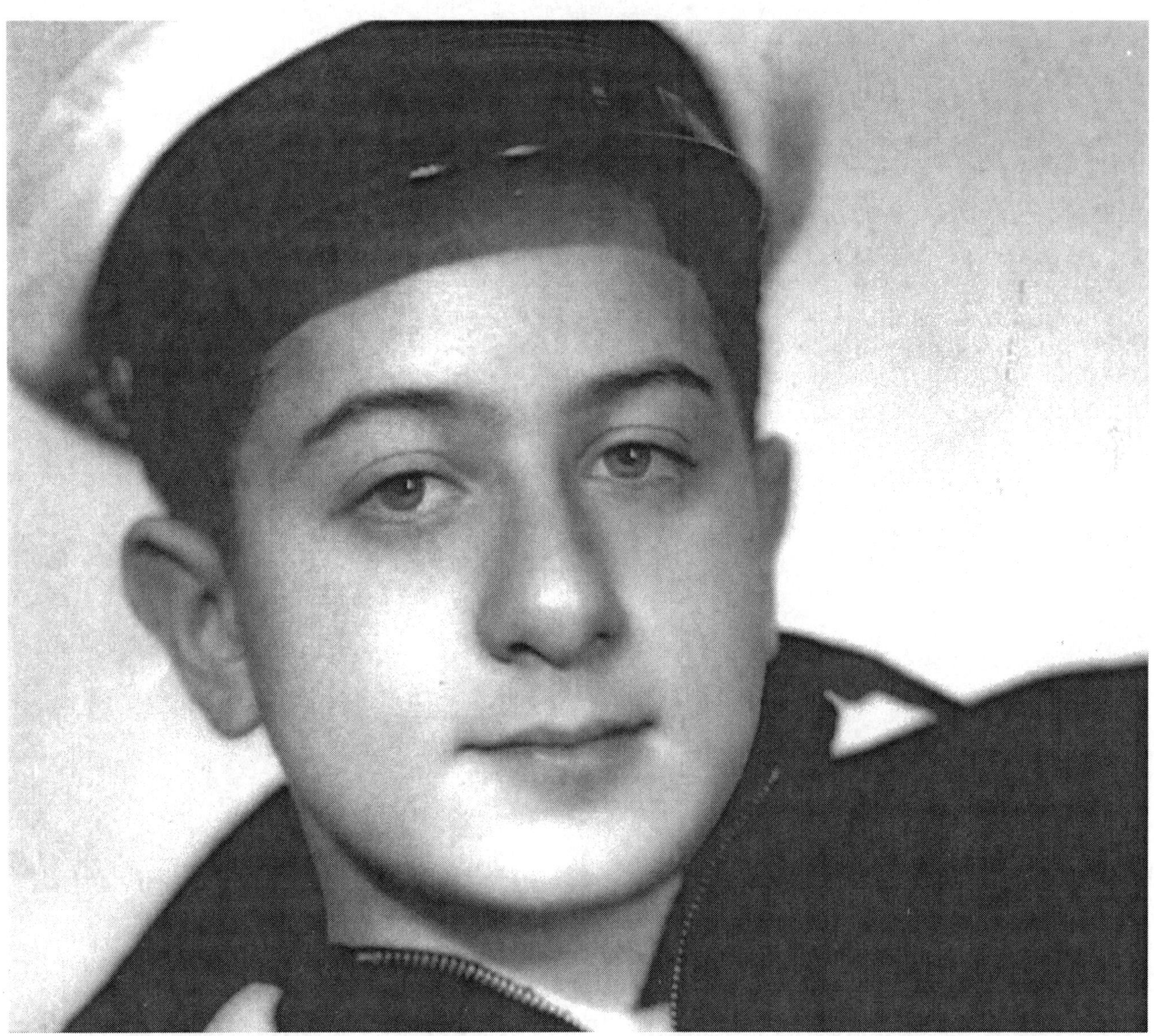

Portrait still of Lester Jay

Portrait still of Marc Lawrence,who worked with the DED, LTG

Portrait still of Sam Edwards

Portrait still of William Tracy

Press photo of a much older Billy Halop

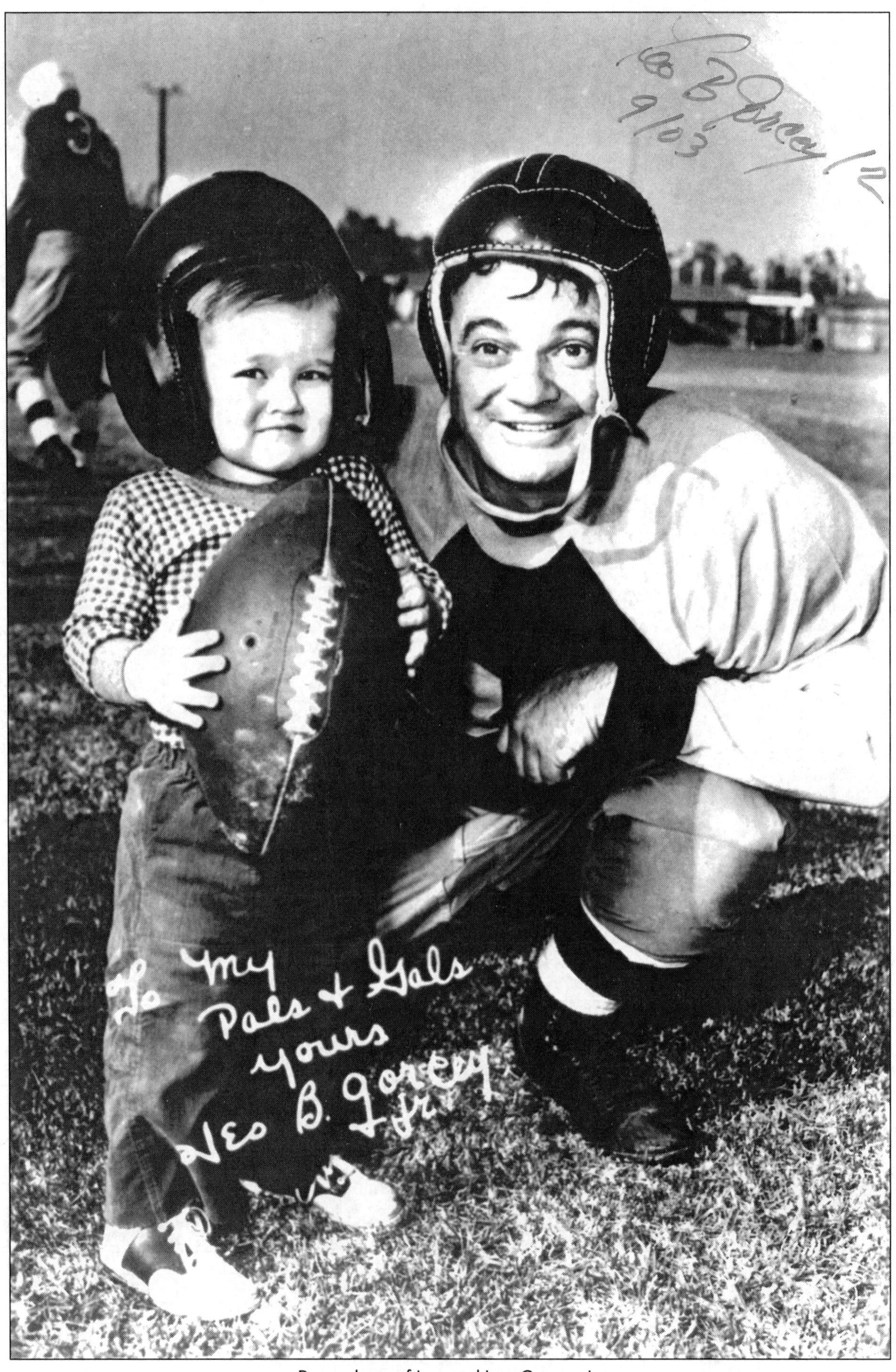

Press photo of Leo and Leo Gorcey Jr.

Press photo of Leo Gorcey and Huntz Hall from the film Dead

Publicity shot from Little Tough Guy

Promo still of the Dead End Kids

Publicity photo of Leo Gorcey, 1945

Publicity portrait of Hally Chester for the film Little Tough Guy

Publicity portrait of Huntz Hall for the film Dead End

Publicity shot of the Dead End Kids

Publicity still for the film Crime School

Publicity still for the film Hell's Kitchen

Publicity still from Crime School

Publicity still from Hell's Kitchen

Publicity still of Bernard Punsly for the film Dead End

Publicity still of Bernard Punsly for the film Give Us Wing

Publicity still of Bernard Punsly

Publicity still of Bill Halop for the film On Dress Parade

Publicity still of Bobby Jordan

Publicity still of Gabe Dell and Leo Gorcey boxing

Publicity still of Harris Berger and Hally Chester

Publicity still of Bill Halop for the film On Dress Parade

Publicity still of Gabe Dell from Jr. G-Men

Publicity still of Joe Turkel, aka Johnny Mutton, in the film Angels in Disguise, Joe was in many Bowery Boys films

Publicity still of John Garfield for the film They Made Me A Criminal

Publicity still of Leo Gorcey from the film Dead End

Publicity still of the Dead End Kids, what are they thinking

Publicity still of the kids on the back lot of Warner Brothers Lot

Publicity still of the kids from the film Hell's Kitchen

Publicity still of the kids from the film They Made Me A Criminal

Publicity still of the kids while they were filming They Made Me A Criminal

Publicity still for the film Crime School

Publicity still of Huntz Hall

Publicity still of Leo Gorcey for the Bowery Boy's film, Bowery Battalion

Publicity still of Leo Gorcey from the film Crime School

Roughing the ball carrier is carried to a new extreme by the Little Tough Guys

Punsly at mic, Dell, Gorcey and Hall

Sammy Morrison

Scene from Delicate Delinquent,Jimmy Murphy 2nd from right

Scene from Angels With Dirty Faces

Scene of the kids from the film Hell's Kitchen

Scene still of Bobby Jordan and Frankie Darro in the film Reformatory

Sea Raiders publicity still

Shot of a young Bobby Jordan

Shot of David Gorcey in the film Little Tough Guys in Society

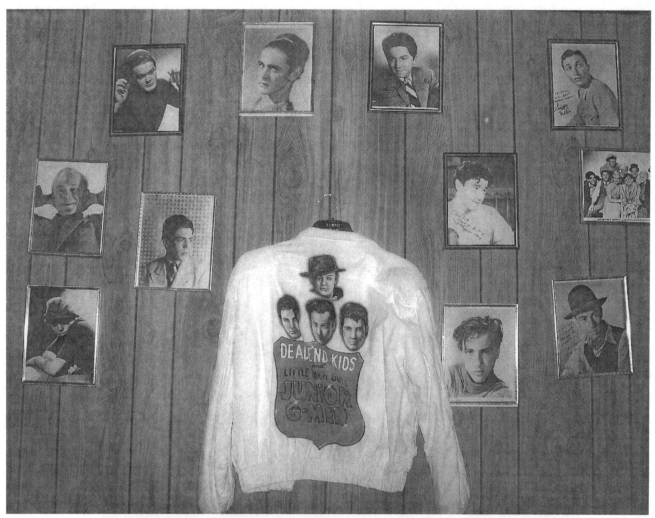

Shot of authors The Dead End Kids room

Shot of Billy Benedict

Shot of Bobby Jordan in the film On Dress Parade

Shot of Bobby Jordan

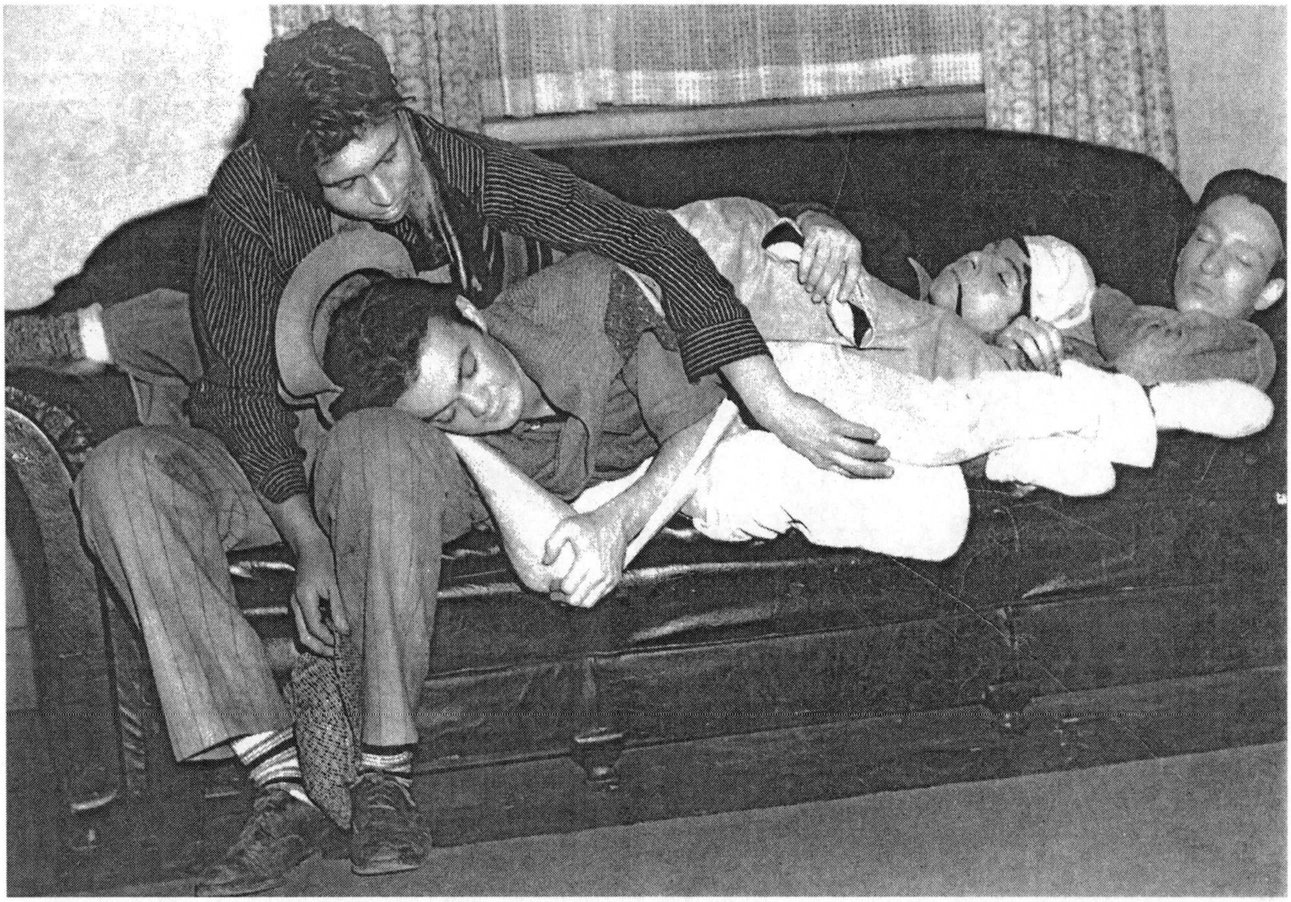

Sleep time in the movies

Shot of East Side Kid Jack Edwards

Shot of Gabe Dell as TB in the play Dead End

Shot of Gorcey in his Bowery Boy days

Shot of Jimmy Lydon

Shot of Leo Gorcey

Sound tec had a difficult task with the kids voices

Staged shot of Universal Studio stars

Stage actor Theodore Newton who played Gimpty in the broadway production of Dead End

HUNTZ HALL
WARNER BROS.
BURBANK, CALIF.

1939

To Richard

Thanks for your lovely letters and support. I am sorry but my photographs haven't arrived yet.

In response to your questions:

my next Picture will be for Ken Russell 'Valente
Staring Rudolph Nurmeyer
Michelle Phillips and myself
I play Jesse L
Head of Studi

Thank you again for your interest, and I hope these answers to your questions are satisfactory to you. If you have any more questions, just write to me at the same address and I will answer promptly.

always
Huntz Hall

P.S. Have you seen my latest picture,

Standered form letter that the Dead End Kids sent out their fans

Stanley Clements and wife (Maria) hold there newly adopted 8 year old son Sylvester while in New York!1964)

Cap-strolling down the ave.

Still of Bernard Gorcey

Still shot of Frankie Thomas from the film Little Tough Guys In Society

Stillof Gabe Dell under contract at Warner Brother's Studio

Sunshine Sammy Morrison

The 2nd ave. Boys

The kids take a break from filming Angels Wash Their Faces

Swing Time in the movies

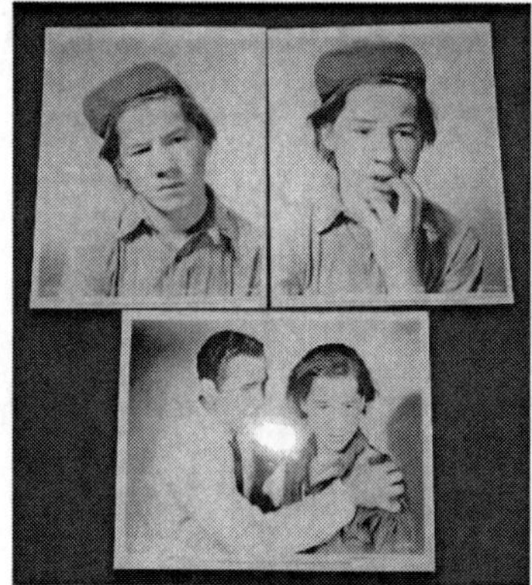

The 3 faces of Bobby Jordan

The Dead End End Kids in a deleted scene from Angels With Dirty Faces

The Dead End Kids are all dressed up and no one to terrorize

The Dead End Kids are all smiles

The Dead End Kids are all smiles in there 1920s swim wear

The Dead End Kids are all smiles when they arrived in Hollywood

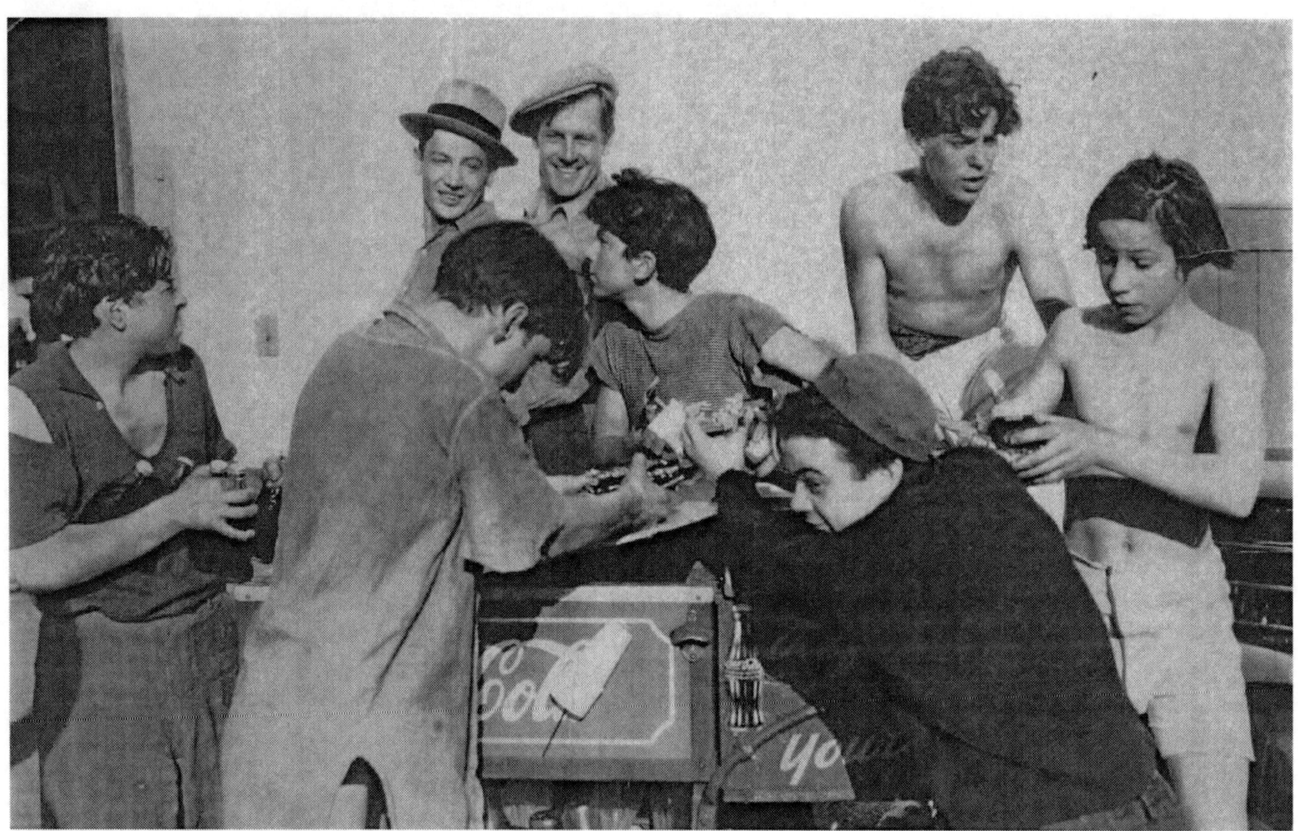

The Dead End Kids are treated to a coke by Joel McCrea while on the set of Dead End

The Dead End Kids arrive in Hollywood from New York

The Dead End Kids get some pointers from director Lewis Seiler

The Dead End Kids horse around on the set of Hell's Kitchen

The Dead End Kids in a deleted scene from the film Crime School

The Dead End Kids make a call with Bogart-Regent 1010

The Dead End Kids rollerskating around the back lot of Warner Brothers

The Dead End Kids take a break from filming

The Dead End Kids strike an unsuspecting pose

The four faces of Eugene Francis

The Kids are all dressed up in this publicity still for the

The Kids get together for a TV show

The kids are all tired out after playing Hockey, in the film Hell's Kitchen

The kids taking on shower after a hard days work

The new Dead End Kids-in Chicago's Griffin Theatre production of Dead End

The Little Tough Guys as they appeared in the film, Little Tough Guys in Society

The Little Tough Guys in a publicity still from the film Code of the Streets

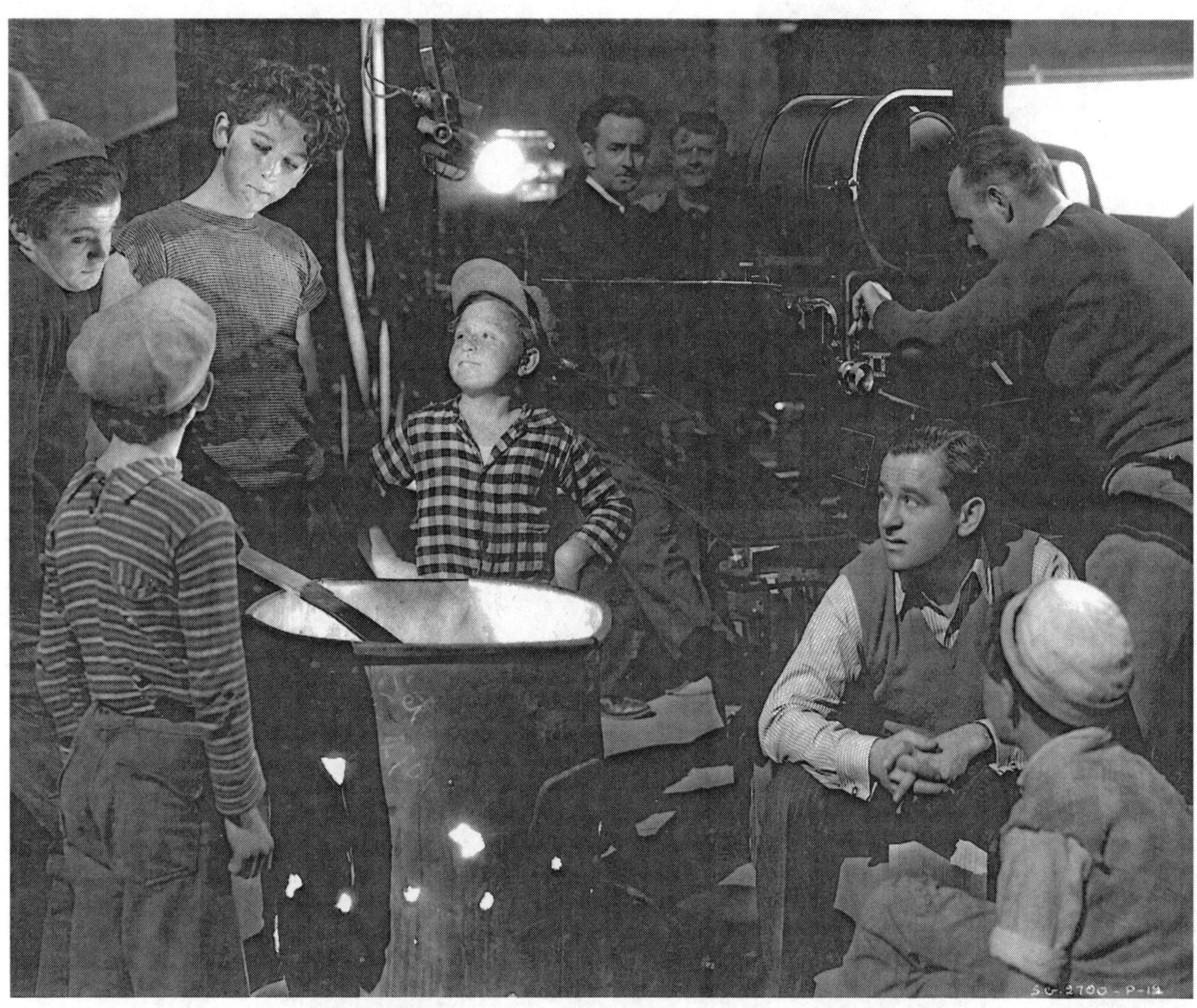

William Wyler keep's a watchful eye on the kids in this still

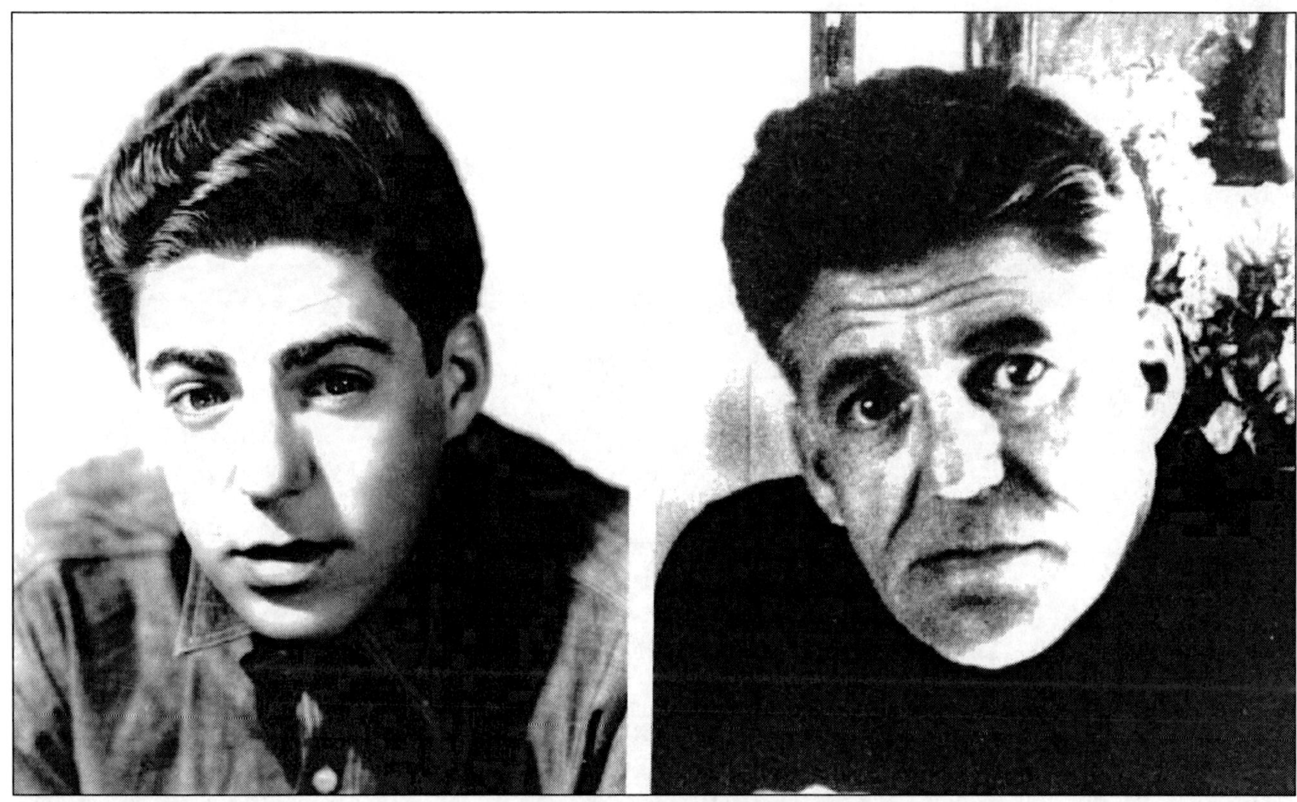

Then and now photos of Billy Halop

Were Dyamite

Top-Abbott, Dell, Jordan, Hall, sit for a pose while filming Keep 'Em Slugging

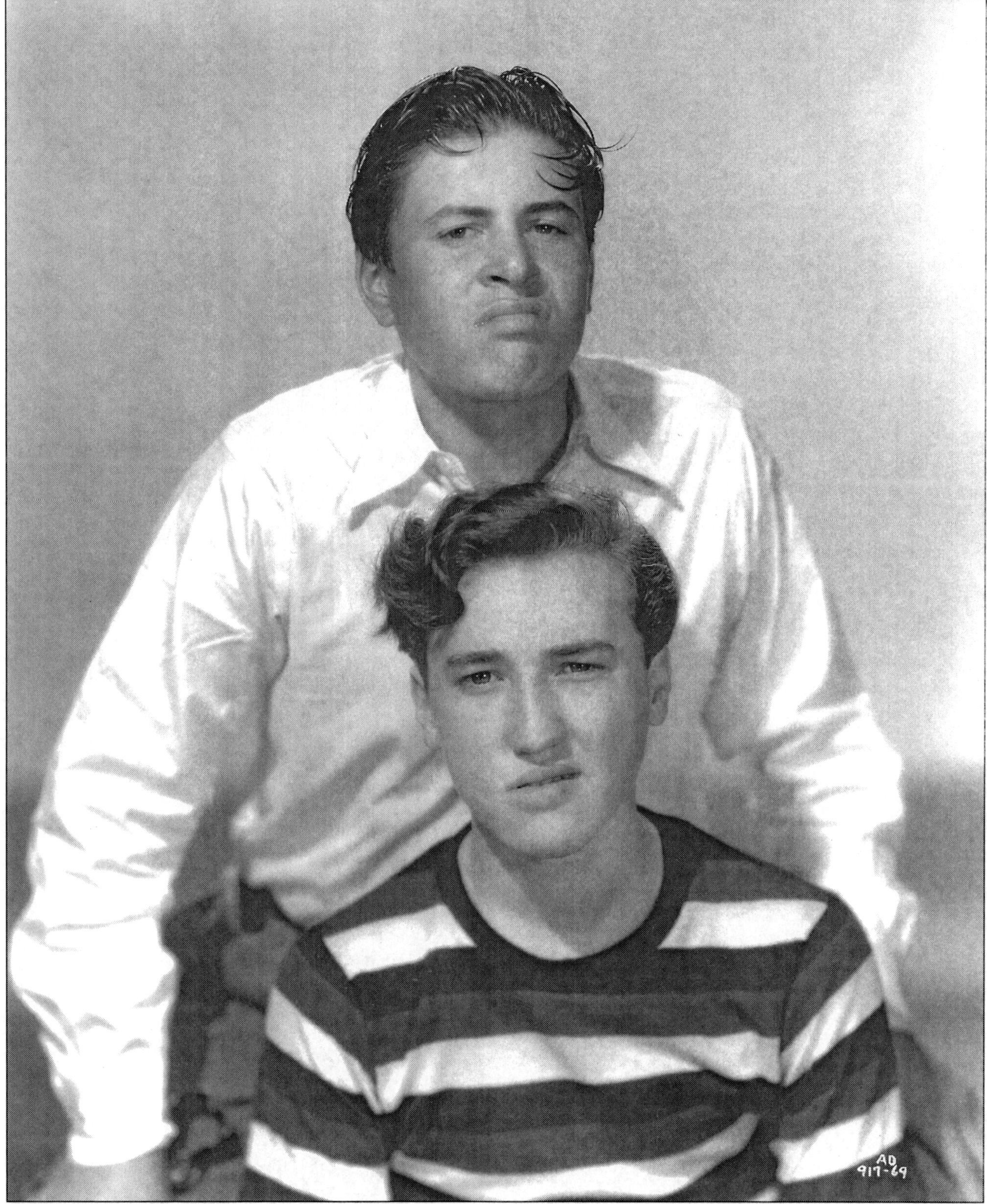

Top, Bernard Punsly (Ape) and Hally Chester (Dopey) in Little Tough Guy

UPI photo of Bobby from March 28th, 1958

Wall photos in Buddy Gormans room

Ward Wood far right in the film Air Force

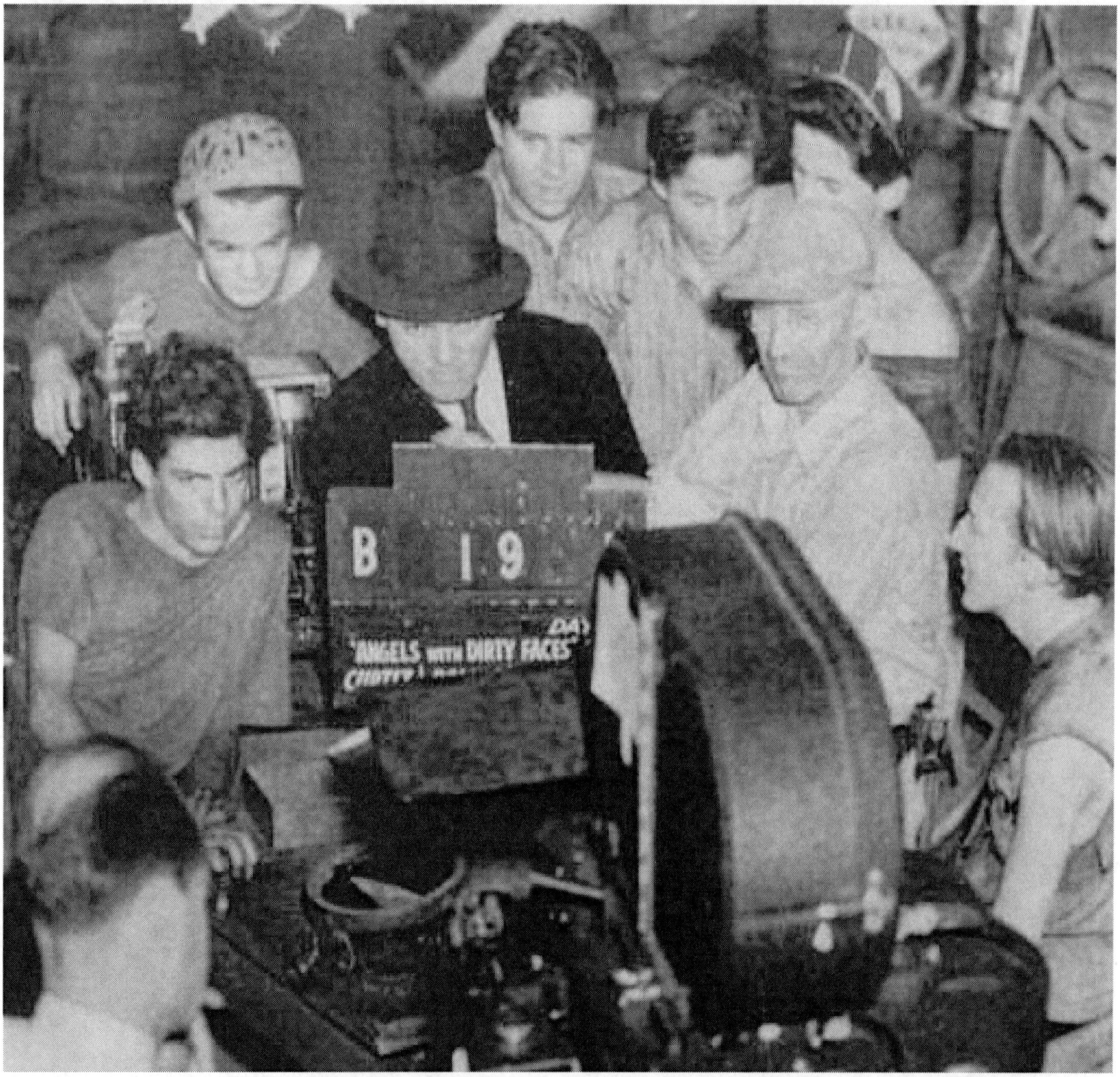

Watching Cagney on the set of Angels With Dirty Faces

William Tracy and Pat O'Brien relaxing on the set of Angels With Dirty Faces

The Little Tough Guys in Little Tough Guys in Society

What lies beneath all these smiles